Essential
SPANISH
VERB
SKILLS

ROGELIO ALONSO VALLECILLOS

McGraw·Hill

New York Chicago San Francisco Lisbon London Madrid Mexico City
Milan New Delhi San Juan Seoul Singapore Sydney Toronto

Library of Congress Cataloging-in-Publication Data

Alonso Vallecillos, Rogelio.
    Essential Spanish verb skills / Rogelio Alonso Vallecillos.
        p.   cm.
    Includes index.
    ISBN 0-07-145390-3
    1. Spanish language—verb.

    PC4271 .A426   2005
    468.2'4—dc22   2005041525

3 4 5 6 7 8 9 0 **DIG/DIG**   0 9

ISBN 0-07-145390-3

Interior design by Nick Panos

McGraw-Hill books are available at special quantity discounts to use as premiums and sales
promotions, or for use in corporate training programs. For more information, please write to the
Director of Special Sales, Professional Publishing, McGraw-Hill, Two Penn Plaza, New York, NY
10121-2298. Or contact your local bookstore.

This book is printed on acid-free paper.

Contents

Introduction

*Y*ou've been studying Spanish for some time now and paid your dues learning how to conjugate verbs. You know how to conjugate verbs in all the tenses and are even comfortable conjugating the most common stem-changing, spelling-changing, and irregular verbs. You've now decided to take the next step in developing a mastery of Spanish verb usage.

No doubt you've noticed that there is much more than just conjugation to understanding how verbs function in context. This is where *Essential Spanish Verb Skills* begins. *Essential Spanish Verb Skills* will show you how to integrate verbs into meaningful sentences.

This book does not deal with basic tense formation since it presupposes that you have already covered this area sufficiently. This approach will save you from having to spend time reexamining what you've already learned. Another very useful feature of this book is that it compares and contrasts how Spanish and English use verbs and tenses. Throughout the book, you will find constant references to how English functions in the particular topic presented, accompanied by clear explanations as to how native Spanish speakers express the same idea.

Essential Spanish Verb Skills offers a wide variety of topics regarding correct verb usage, in particular areas that often cause a lot of difficulty for English-speaking students. The book's clear explanations are supplemented by thorough examples. Each chapter also includes a variety of exercises that will enable you to practice and reinforce what you have just learned. Moreover, at the end of the book you will find a handy appendix of Quick-Glance Tables that will provide you with quick and practical clarifications of a number of important verb topics.

By the time you finish this book, you will find yourself well on your way to speaking and writing in Spanish better than ever. *¡Buena suerte!*

Ser and *Estar*

You have probably encountered already the two verbs that mean *to be*: **ser** and **estar**. Both are notoriously difficult for learners of Spanish to master. Even though these verbs follow established rules, it is not easy to become proficient in their usage without understanding the specific situations that determine their use. Explaining the differences between the two is not easy either, since both verbs have the same meaning in English. A basic rule is that **ser** describes qualities or characteristics inherent to the person, animal, or thing talked about, and **estar** describes temporary qualities or characteristics, states, location, situation, etc. Since this general rule may not be enough to master the topic, this chapter offers an extensive selection of examples as well as many specific and often confusing situations to help you make the right choice.

Ser

The verb **ser** is related to characteristics that say what somebody/something is like and what somebody/something has become. It is also connected with the idea of acting as somebody/something. **Ser** is used:

- To indicate profession/occupation. In this case, it is not important whether the profession/occupation is temporary or not:

Yo soy profesor.	I am a teacher.
Tú eres médico.	You are a doctor.
Él no es mecánico.	He is not a mechanic.
Ella no es enfermera.	She is not a nurse.
Nosotros somos abogados.	We are lawyers.

- To designate people, animals, and things:

Juan es mi hermano.	Juan is my brother.
Ella es la jefa.	She is the boss.
Ellos son Pedro y Laura.	They are Pedro and Laura.
No es un perro.	It is not a dog.

- To indicate fixed qualities/characteristics inherent to the person, animal, or thing described:

Ana es muy guapa.	Ana is very beautiful.
El coche es muy caro.	The car is very expensive.
Carlos es muy inteligente.	Carlos is very intelligent.

- To say when or where something takes place, even if the event takes place only once:

Las clases de inglés son los lunes.	English classes are on Mondays.
La fiesta es mañana.	The party is tomorrow.
La clase de inglés es en mi casa.	The English class is in my house.

- To say what something is for:

Esto es para corregir exámenes.	This is (used) for marking exams.
Eso es para lavar ropa.	That is (used) for washing clothes.

Estar

The verb **estar** is generally used to describe being/staying somewhere and characteristics/qualities that are not considered to be permanent. Therefore, **estar** is used:

- To talk about position/location/situation:

Los dormitorios están arriba.	The bedrooms are upstairs.
El coche no está en el garaje.	The car is not in the garage.

Estamos en una situación muy difícil.	We are in a very difficult situation.

- To talk about states, qualities and characteristics that are considered temporary:

Yo estoy asustado.	I am scared.
Ella no está casada.	She is not married.
Ellos están nerviosos.	They are nervous.
Él está preocupado.	He is worried.
Laura no está enfadada.	Laura is not angry.

- To refer to health situations, even if the person described has no possible cure (including *being dead* = **estar muerto**). The same occurs with nouns and adjectives that refer to health in general, especially when the adjective ends in **-ado/-ido**:

Yo estoy enfermo.	I am sick.
Ese hombre está loco.	That man is crazy.
Ella está embarazada.	She is pregnant.
Mi tío está alcoholizado.	My uncle is an alcoholic.

But health adjectives ending in **-ico** usually need the verb **ser**:

Mi tío es alcohólico.	My uncle is an alcoholic.

Specific Uses

Apart from the general uses described, the verbs **ser** and **estar** have their specific uses in tense construction. A very important use is the passive, where only **ser** is possible:

La casa fue pintada el año pasado.	The house was painted last year.
El puente será construido pronto.	The bridge will be built soon.
Esto no va a ser vendido.	This is not going to be sold.
El ladrón ha sido arrestado.	The thief has been arrested.

But be careful with so-called semipassive sentences, which always use the verb *estar*. These are constructions in which the past participle has the function of an adjective. In fact, semipassive sentences indicate a situation, not an action. Compare:

La puerta es abierta. (passive)   The door is open<u>ed</u>.
La puerta está abierta.   The door is op<u>en</u>.
  (semipassive)

In translating English sentences in which phrasal verbs (i.e., those with prepositions) are used, the difference between semipassive and true passive constructions is much easier to see:

La tele es encendida.   The TV is turned on.
La tele está encendida.   The TV is on.

With adjectives/past participles that refer to the material something is made of, both verbs are possible, but *estar* is much more common:

Eso está hecho de plástico.   That is made of plastic.

When referring to the place where something is made, both verbs can be used. The choice between one verb and the other is, in these cases, purely subjective; if the speaker wants to emphasize the production process (a true passive), *ser* is used; if the speaker is only thinking of the place or the material, *estar* is preferable:

*En Alemania, los coches son   In Germany, cars are made under
  fabricados bajo muy estrictas   very strict norms.
  normas.*
*Estas alfombras están hechas en   These carpets are made in Iran.
  Irán.*

Only the verb *estar* is possible when forming progressive, or continuous, tenses:

Estamos comiendo.   We are eating.
Ellos no están durmiendo.   They are not sleeping.

Note: The verb **estar** is followed by participles (not gerunds) when position is referred to. These participles function as real adjectives:

Ella está sentada.	She is sitting/seated.
Juan está tumbado en el suelo.	John is lying on the floor.

The English verb *to stand* translates as **estar de pie**:

Ellos están de pie.	They are standing.

In saying what somebody/something is for, **ser** is used, but when the meaning conveys being in the mood for, up to doing something, or having enough energy, only **estar** is possible. Compare:

Esto es para abrir agujeros.	This is (used) for making holes.
Este autobús es para el transporte escolar.	This bus is (used) for school transportation.
No estoy para fiestas.	I'm not in the mood for parties.
Este coche no está para un largo viaje.	This car is not up for (making) a long trip.

Confusing Cases

There are many cases in which both verbs are possible, often with a difference of meaning. The most important ones are dealt with here:

To express that there has been a change in qualities or characteristics, the verb **estar** is used, even if the change implies a definitive quality:

Roberto está muy alto.	Roberto is very tall.
Roberto es muy alto.	Roberto is very tall.

The first sentence is talking about Robert's change. Some time ago he was quite short and now he is very tall. The second sentence only states that Robert "owns" the quality of being tall. The person who uses **está** must have known Robert for some time. Very often, when talking about a child's height (or other physical characteristics), the verb **estar** is used, even if the child is a complete stranger. The reason is that children are growing and changing all the time.

In descriptions in general (physical, social, marital, economic, etc.), *estar* only refers to the moment the speaker is talking about. Here are some important examples:

María está muy guapa.	María is very beautiful.
María es muy guapa.	María is very beautiful.

The first sentence just means that María *looks* beautiful. Maybe she has changed, maybe she hasn't. Perhaps she is wearing wonderful clothes that make her look beautiful. In the speaker's mind, *estar* refers to just now, right at this moment (or around this moment). The second sentence is only a confirmation of María's usual beauty.

Juan está soltero.	Juan is single/unmarried.
Juan es soltero.	Juan is single/unmarried.

The first sentence is a reference to Juan's present situation. The second sentence is qualifying Juan as somebody who is unmarried. The same applies to *viudo* (*widower*) and *viuda* (*widow*), but with *casado* (*married*), *estar* is preferable, although *ser* is possible.

Pedro está rico.	Pedro is rich.
Pedro es rico.	Pedro is rich.

The first sentence is a reference to Pedro's present situation (maybe as a result of a change). The second sentence only says that Pedro is a wealthy man.

Él está tonto.	He is (being) stupid.
Él es tonto.	He is stupid.

In the first sentence, he is acting stupidly. The second sentence means that he lacks intelligence.

Yo estoy gordo.	I am fat.
Yo soy gordo.	I am fat.

The first sentence is a reference to my present situation. The second one implies that I am fat because I have been fat all my life (or for a very long time). When talking about people, **estar** is much more common with the adjectives **delgado** and **gordo**, even if the person being described is a complete stranger. When referring to things, use **ser** with the adjectives **delgado/fino** and **grueso/gordo**.

When a noun is qualified by an adjective (i.e., noun and adjective together), only the verb **ser** can be used:

Ella es una mujer muy alta.	She is a very tall woman.
Tú eres un hombre casado.	You are a married man.

Spanish adjectives can be made into nouns by putting articles before them. When this is the case, only **ser** is possible:

Ella es la más alta.	She is the tallest.
Él es el gordo que está en el rincón.	He is the fat one who is in the corner.

With adverbs, **estar** is used. Compare:

Él es bueno.	He is good.
Él está bien.	He is well.

Since **ser** is used with fixed characteristics and **estar** with temporary ones, compare the following two sentences:

¿Cómo es ella?	What is she like?
¿Cómo está ella?	How is she?

Es asks for a description. **Está** asks about her present situation. In both cases **cómo** is used, while English needs to use *what . . . like* and *how* in order to make a clear distinction in the speaker's intentions.

English adjectives ending in *-ing* (e.g., *boring, exciting, amazing*) are used with the verb **ser**. English adjectives ending in *-ed* (e.g., *bored, excited, amazed*) are used with **estar**:

Este libro es muy interesante.	This book is very interesting.
Estoy interesado en ese libro.	I am interested in that book.
Ella es aburrida.	She is boring.
Ella está aburrida.	She is bored.

When talking about possession, only the verb *ser* is possible, even if the possession is temporary:

Ahora este coche es mío.	Now this car is mine.
Ella ya no es la mujer de Tony.	She is no longer Tony's wife.

Opinions about something that has happened or about something that is being explained require the verb *ser*:

Eso es raro.	That is strange.
Es incomprensible.	It is incomprehensible.

But the adjective ***claro*** (*clear*), meaning that the speaker understands the situation or the explanation, needs the verb ***estar***:

Eso está claro.	That is clear./I understand.

Exercise 1

Write the correct form of the present tense of the verb ***ser*** or ***estar***. If both verbs are possible, include both of them.

1. Mis hermanos _____ en Madrid en este momento.

2. La madre de Pepe _____ ama de casa.

3. Yo _____ muy nervioso en este momento, aunque yo no _____ nervioso por naturaleza.

4. Tu hermana _____ muy delgada.

5. Los padres de Antonio _____ en Inglaterra de vacaciones.

6. La fiesta _____ en la casa de María.

7. Ella _____ muy bien, gracias.

8. ¿_____ usted de América?

9. ¿_____ ustedes casados?

10. ¡(Tú) _____ muy guapa esta noche!

Exercise 2
Underline the correct option.

1. Ana *es/está* soltera, pero Carlos *es/está* viudo.

2. ¿A qué hora *son/están* los exámenes?

3. ¿A qué hora *son/están* ustedes en casa?

4. Juan *es/está* mi mejor amigo.

5. Ella *es/está* la mejor de mi clase.

6. Yo *soy/estoy* aburrido, porque la película *es/está* aburrida.

7. Nosotros *somos/estamos* en una mala situación.

8. La puerta *es/está* abierta.

9. Ese coche *es/está* de mi hermano.

10. Ella *es/está* alta, rubia y muy simpática.

Exercise 3
Correct any mistakes.

1. ¿Cómo son tus padres? ¿Son bien? _____

2. La tienda está cerrada porque es muy tarde. _____

3. Esos coches son fabricados en Alemania. _____

4. Es nublado, pero no es lloviendo. _____

5. Eso que tú estás diciendo no está comprensible. _____

6. Esta noche yo soy libre, así que podemos ir al cine. _____

7. Ella es libre. Puede casarse con quien quiera. _____

8. La mujer que es de pie es mi madre. _____

9. ¿Por qué eres (tú) tumbado? _____

10. ¿Por qué está Pablo cerrando la cochera? _____

Infinitive or Gerund

With the exception of the verb **estar**, which is usually followed by gerunds or adjectives, and a few other cases that will be covered later in this chapter, only infinitives can appear after a verb. This means that Spanish doesn't make a distinction between *to* and *-ing* constructions as in the sentences *I want <u>to be</u> a doctor* and *I like <u>being</u> a doctor*. In Spanish, any verb that comes after another verb (except for the cases that follow) must be in the infinitive form and will, therefore, end in **-ar**, **-er**, or **-ir**:

Yo quiero comer.	I want to eat.
Ella no puede estar aquí.	She can't be here.
Tú debes evitar comer chocolate.	You must avoid eating chocolate.
¿Te importa cerrar la ventana?	Do you mind closing the window?
No soporto estar con ese hombre.	I can't stand being with that man.

Both the infinitive and the gerund can be used at the beginning of a sentence, but there is usually an important difference of meaning:

Comer así es peligroso.	Eating like that is dangerous.
Comiendo así engordarás.	If you eat like that, you will get fat.

The following rules deal with this problematic area:

The Gerund

When the verb *estar* is used, gerunds or adjectives must follow:

Ella no puede estar durmiendo.	She can't be sleeping.
La tienda debe estar abierta.	The store must be open.

A great number of the adjectives that follow the verb *estar* are past participles:

Él está ido.	He is crazy.
Estás un poco bebido.	You are a little drunk.
Estamos preparados.	We are ready.

After verbs that imply feelings that range from pleasure to suffering, gerunds must be used:

Yo disfruto estudiando idiomas.	I enjoy learning languages.
Ella goza montando en bicicleta.	She enjoys riding a bike.

Gerunds must follow any verb when indicating *how* something is obtained or done, and to express that the action represented by the gerund *is still taking place*:

Yo practico hablando con la gente.	I practice by (means of) talking with people.
Puedes conseguir eso trabajando más.	You can get/obtain that by (means of) working harder.
Ella vino hablando conmigo.	She was talking with me while we were coming.
El profesor continuó hablando.	The teacher went on talking.

Compare the following two examples:

Lo conseguí hablando.	I got/obtained it by (means of) talking.
Conseguí hablar con él.	I managed to talk with him.

In the first example, the speaker obtained something by means of an action. In the second example, the speaker succeeded in something.

The gerund can appear at the beginning of a clause. In this position, its function indicates that something happens while/when something else is taking place:

Yendo por la calle encontré esto.	I found this (while I was) walking down the street.
Viniendo al pueblo tuvimos un accidente.	We had an accident (when we were) coming to the village.

The order of this kind of sentence can be inverted, so that the part in which the gerund appears becomes the complement of the other part: ***Encontré esto yendo por la calle*** and ***Tuvimos un accidente viniendo al pueblo.***

In general, the gerund is used at the beginning of clauses as long as it is not the subject of the sentence. Compare:

Conducir así es muy peligroso.	Driving like that is very dangerous.
Conduciendo así tendrás un accidente.	You will have an accident (if you keep) driving like that.

In the first case, the subject of the sentence is ***conducir***. In the second case, the subject is the subject pronoun ***tú***, which has been omitted.

In giving directions, the gerund is often used:

Entrando a la derecha está el bar./El bar está entrando a la derecha.

This sentence means that *if you walk in and turn to the right, you will find the bar.* Be careful with the second version, as you might think that the gerund is used because the verb ***está*** is placed before it. This coincidence could make you think that the sentence says that *the bar is walking in.*

The gerund often expresses nuances that depend on the speaker's intentions and the context:

Ella llegó a casa <u>diciendo</u> que había tenido un accidente.	She came home <u>and said</u> that she had had an accident.
<u>Terminando</u> esto podremos ir a la playa.	<u>As soon as we finish</u> this we will be able to go to the beach.

Ellos compraron la casa, vendiéndola dos meses más tarde.	They bought the house <u>and sold</u> it two months later.
Telefoneé a mis padres pidiéndoles dinero.	I telephoned my parents <u>asking them</u> for money.
Estando él en casa, mi madre está feliz.	<u>If he is</u> at home, my mother is happy.
Aun no siendo guapa, me enamoré de ella.	<u>Although she wasn't</u> beautiful, I fell in love with her.
Tengo un hijo estudiando en la universidad.	I have a son <u>(who is) studying</u> in college.
Hay un profesor explicando la lección.	There is a teacher <u>(who is) explaining</u> the lesson.

The Infinitive

With the exception of the cases previously stated, and of the verb **haber** (*to have*) as in **He comprado una casa** (*I have bought a house*), only infinitives can follow a verb in Spanish and only infinitives can be the subject of a sentence:

Me encanta comer caracoles.	I love eating snails.
Ella odia trabajar en la cocina.	She hates working in the kitchen.
Necesito vender esta casa.	I need to sell this house.
Debo hacer mis ejercicios.	I must do my exercises.
Ir allí es muy peligroso.	Going there is very dangerous.

Only the infinitive can form a construction with **al** (contraction of the preposition **a** and the article **el**) to mean *on/in + -ing*:

al entrar	on entering
al explicar esto	in explaining this

This important construction (**al** + infinitive) is often used to mean that something happens while/when something else is taking place (or that an action takes place as a result of something):

Al verme, (ella) se marchó.	She left when she saw me.

The infinitive can be followed by the subject pronoun, but then the pronoun of the next verb must be omitted, unless both actions are done by different subjects:

Al llamarla yo, ella se puso nerviosa.	She got nervous when I called her.

Al + infinitive can also be used to indicate where something is:

Al salir del banco hay un kiosco.	There is a kiosk outside the bank.

Spanish uses only infinitives after prepositions:

Gracias por ayudarme.	Thank you for helping me.
Ella insistió en venir con nosotros.	She insisted on coming with us.

Verbs that imply actions connected with the senses can be followed by either the infinitive or the gerund. The gerund is more advisable when the action referred to has not been completed:

Vi a Pedro limpiando/limpiar la cocina.	I saw Pedro cleaning the kitchen.
No les oí entrar.	I didn't hear them come in.

Note: The verb ***haber***, used in the conjugation of perfect tenses, can only be followed by past participles:

Yo no he comido.	I haven't eaten.
Ella ha estado corriendo.	She has been running.
No hemos comprado nada.	We haven't bought anything.

Exercise 1

Put the verbs in parentheses into the gerund or infinitive.

1. A Elena le encanta _____ (pasear) en la lluvia.

2. ¿Te importa _____ (dejar) la puerta abierta?

3. _____ (entrar) en la ciudad vi un terrible accidente.

4. Necesito _____ (terminar) esto antes del lunes.

5. Ellos están _____ (terminar) de _____ (hacer) un examen.

6. ¿Por qué no intentas _____ (hablar) con él? A veces puede _____ (ser) razonable.

7. _____ (pintar) de esa forma no vas a _____ (conseguir) _____ (acabar) para esta noche.

8. María está a punto de _____ (tener) un bebé.

9. _____ (salir) del cine me di cuenta de que había dejado mi paraguas dentro.

10. _____ (salir) de mi casa a la derecha hay un buen restaurante.

Exercise 2

Fill in the blanks with the infinitive or gerund of the verbs that follow. The verbs can be used more than once.

discutir	hacer	trabajar
ser	hablar	ahorrar
salir	jugar	ver

1. _____ con desconocidos es peligroso.

2. No tiene sentido _____ con la policía.

3. Ella dio un grito al _____ que había un hombre en su habitación.

4. Has ganado _____ trampas.

5. Hemos conseguido _____ algo de dinero _____ mucho.

6. Fuimos a _____ las nuevas condiciones.

7. Fuimos _____ todo el rato. Ella estaba realmente enfadada.

8. Les oí _____ del robo.

9. Ella no nos quiso ver _____ al tenis.

10. _____ o no _____ , ésa es la cuestión.

Exercise 3
Underline the correct option.

1. Antonio nos llamó para *decirnos/diciéndonos* que no podía venir.

2. Felipe me llamó *decir/diciendo* que su madre estaba enferma.

3. *Hacer/Haciendo* tus deberes podrás ver la televisión.

4. Ellos no me quieren *dejar/dejando ver/viendo* su colección de sellos.

5. Tendrás que *seguir/siguiendo trabajar/trabajando* para mí.

6. Intento *empujar/empujando* el coche cuesta arriba.

7. Sugiero *hablar/hablando* con el director primero.

Exercise 4
Correct any mistakes.

1. Estoy muy cansando y necesito dormir un poco.

   _____

2. No vale la pena hablando con ella. _____

3. He aumentado mi capital invertir en bolsa. _____

4. La luz de tu dormitorio está encendiendo. _____

5. Por no haciendo los ejercicios, el maestro me castigó.

   _____

6. Salvé a los ocupantes romper el cristal. _____

7. La tienda está cerrada. Si te das prisa, podrás comprando la leche.

   _____

8. Lo siento, usted no está capacitando para ocupar ese puesto.

   _____

9. Me gustaría pudiendo hacer eso. _____

10. Tocando cables de alto voltaje puede ser fatal. _____

Simple Present and Present Continuous

Although there are important similarities between English and Spanish with regard to the use of these two tenses, there are also significant differences that deserve specific coverage. Here are some ways in which these Spanish tenses differ from English language usage.

The Present Tense

The Spanish present tense of the indicative (***presente de indicativo***) has a much wider use than its counterpart in English. It is used:

- To talk about habits or events that happen regularly, facts, future arrangements, intentions, etc. In fact, continuous, or progressive, forms (i.e., tenses with gerunds) are never used to express future plans, arrangements, or intentions:

Ella habla español muy bien.	She speaks Spanish very well.
Mañana voy a Los Ángeles.	I'm going to Los Angeles tomorrow.
La Tierra gira alrededor del sol.	The Earth turns around the sun.
Ella viene mañana.	She is coming tomorrow.
Yo nunca como allí.	I never eat there.
Nosotros vivimos en Madrid.	We live in Madrid.
¿Fumas?	Do you smoke?
La semana que viene no trabajo.	I'm not working next week.

- To talk about decisions taken at the moment of speaking. In these cases, English uses the future:

  Carla: *El teléfono está sonando.*   The phone is ringing.
  Tony: *Yo lo cojo.*   I'll pick it up.

- To talk about future activities that are scheduled or depend on time tables:

  ¿A qué hora empieza la película?   What time does the film start?
  ¿A qué hora abren las tiendas?   What time do the stores open?

- To make proposals/suggestions of the type *"shall I/shall we . . . ?"*:

  ¿Te ayudo?   Shall I help you?
  ¿Qué compro?   What shall I buy?
  ¿Dónde comemos?   Where shall we eat?

- To talk about actions that are taking place at the moment of speaking:

  Hola, Juan, ¿qué haces?   Hi, Juan, what are you doing?
  ¿Qué comes?   What are you eating?
  ¿Dónde vas?   Where are you going?

The Present Continuous

The present continuous is almost exclusively used to talk about actions that are taking place *at* or *around* the moment of speaking:

Ella está estudiando.   She is studying.
Ellos no están durmiendo.   They are not sleeping.
¿Estás leyendo un libro?   Are you reading a book?
Está nevando.   It is snowing.
Estoy dando clases de conducir.   I'm giving driving lessons.

The simple present can also be used in these examples.

Similarly to English, there are many Spanish verbs that are not acceptable in continuous tenses. These are usually verbs that are not connected with the idea of physical activity. Fortunately for English-speaking students, these verbs generally coincide with those English verbs that don't usually accept progressive forms. Here are some examples:

Ahora no tengo tiempo.	I haven't got any time now.
Ella me conoce muy bien.	She knows me very well.
No me gusta esta película.	I don't like this film.
Pienso que ella es culpable.	I think that she is guilty.
Creo que él vive en Londres.	I believe that he lives in London.
Odio los deberes.	I hate homework.
Ahora prefiero tomar una cerveza.	Now I prefer to have a beer.
Ella se parece a su padre.	She looks like her father.
Te debo la vida.	I owe you my life.
¿Cuánto cuesta eso?	How much does that cost?

But some of these stative verbs (i.e., those that express a state, condition, or relation rather than an action) can be used in the progressive, or continuous, tense in Spanish, especially when the process during which the action is taking place is referred to:

Eso me está costando una fortuna.	That has cost me a fortune (so far).
No me está gustando la película.	I don't like the movie (what I have seen so far).

In many cases, English and Spanish have similar uses:

Pienso que esto es muy caro.	I think that this is very expensive.
Estoy pensando en ti todo el tiempo. *Pienso en ti todo el tiempo.*	I'm thinking of you all the time.
Tengo una casa en España.	I have a house in Spain.
Estamos teniendo problemas con ella. *Tenemos problemas con ella.*	We are having problems with her.

Simple or Continuous

The use of the simple present and the present continuous can be rather confusing in many cases. Sometimes they are both correct, despite the fact that Spanish speakers have certain preferences; in other cases, the use of one tense or the other implies significant differences.

In Spanish, both the simple present and the present continuous can be used to talk about something that is happening at the moment of speaking:

Hola, ¿qué haces?	Hello, what are you doing?
Hola, ¿qué estás haciendo?	
Veo la tele.	I'm watching TV.
Estoy viendo la tele.	

Generally, the continuous tense sounds more natural when referring to the moment of speaking, especially in answering questions or giving additional information. This means that ***Estoy viendo la tele*** is a little better.

The verbs ***ir*** (*to go*) and ***venir*** (*to come*) rarely admit progressive, or continuous, tenses when talking about actions that are taking place at the moment of speaking:

Hola, ¿dónde vas?	Hello, where are you going?
(Not: *Hola, ¿dónde estás yendo?*)	
Voy al banco.	I'm going to the bank.
(Not: *Estoy yendo al banco.*)	

These verbs are only used in the continuous, or progressive, tense when attention is being paid to the movement itself:

Ahora están yendo hacia la iglesia.	Now they are going/walking towards the church.
Los invitados están viniendo hacia aquí.	The guests are coming here.

The simple present can be used in these two examples, but as the action is already taking place, the continuous tense is better. A sentence like ***Ahora vienen*** can mean that *they intend to come now* or that *they are on* *their way now* (confusing), but the sentence **Están viniendo** can only mean that *they are on their way*. Despite this, it is advisable to use simple tenses with the verbs *ir* and *venir* because, depending on adverbs and clauses that are added, their continuous tenses don't always sound correct. For example, **ya vienen** can only mean that *they are on their way*.

The construction *ir a* + infinitive and the English construction *to be going to* + verb both express the same thing:

Ella va a venir.	She is going to come.
¿Va usted a beber algo?	Are you going to drink something?
Va a llover.	It is going to rain.

The phrase *ir a* can never be used in the continuous tense when referring to the future. A sentence like **Ella está yendo a venir** is impossible.

In general, questions with interrogatives (**qué**, **dónde**, **cómo**, etc.) are correct in both the simple present and the present continuous, but the answers to these questions sound more natural in the present continuous:

¿Qué comes?/¿Qué estás comiendo?	What are you eating?
Como pan./Estoy comiendo pan.	I'm eating bread.

With the adverb **siempre** (*always*), the continuous tense is preferable when the sentence denotes irritation or pleasure (the simple present is possible, but less advisable):

¡Siempre estás hablando de fútbol!	You're always talking about football!
Él es muy amable. Siempre está ayudando.	He is very kind. He is always helping.

This doesn't usually happen with the adverb **nunca** (*never*):

Nunca me prestas tu auto. (Not: *Nunca me estás prestando tu auto.*)	You never lend me your car.
¡Nunca cenas en casa!	You never have dinner at home!

When talking about development, growth, etc., both tenses can be used, but the continuous is better:

Los precios están subiendo todo el tiempo.	Prices are going up all the time.
Mis niños están creciendo muy rápido.	My children are growing very fast.

For habitual situations, facts, etc., the simple present is almost always used:

El Támesis desemboca en el Atlántico.	The Thames flows into the Atlantic Ocean.
Ella vive en este pueblo.	She lives in this town.
El agua hierve a los 100 grados.	Water boils at 100 degrees.
Mi padre escribe novelas.	My father writes novels.

Sometimes the continuous tense can be used in these cases, especially with adverbs and adverbials that normally go with the present continuous, when the situation is considered to be temporary or very recent, or when the idea of change or correction is present:

Ahora estoy viviendo con mis padres.	Now I'm living with my parents.
Ahora vivo con mis padres.	
Ella está trabajando en un banco.	She is working in a bank.
Ella trabaja en un banco.	

Living with my parents can be a habit, but if I'm living with my parents now as a result of my divorce, I am talking about a situation which is either temporary or one with a recent start. It can even be a correction because the person who is talking with me thought (or might think) that my situation was different. Working in a bank can be a habitual situation, but if I am talking about a woman who used to work in a store and changed jobs, I introduce the correction or express the change by means of the continuous tense. It is even possible that she is working in that bank temporarily.

There is a verb in Spanish that emphasizes the idea of habit. It is the stem-changing verb **soler**, which changes the **o** in the stem to **ue**, except in the ***nosotros*** and ***vosotros*** forms of the present. In English, this verb only exists in the past (*used to*). To express habits, English uses the simple present with adverbs of frequency. In Spanish, ***soler*** is always followed by the infinitive:

Yo suelo salir los sábados.	I usually go out on Saturdays.
Ella no suele trabajar de noche.	She doesn't usually work at night.

The sentences ***Yo usualmente/normalmente salgo los sábados*** and ***Ella usualmente/normalmente no trabaja de noche*** are possible as well.

For actions *around* the moment of speaking, the present continuous is preferable:

Estoy leyendo un libro muy bueno.	I'm reading a very good book. (*Maybe I'm not reading at this moment, but having coffee with a friend.*)

With proposals and suggestions of the type *shall I/shall we*, and with decisions taken at the moment of speaking (where *will* is used in English), only the simple present is possible:

De acuerdo. Yo voy.	All right. I'll go.
¿Te ayudo?	Shall I help you?
¿Qué le compro?	What shall I buy him?

In expressing future arrangements, plans, and intentions, only the simple present is possible:

Mañana veo a Pedro.	I'm seeing Pedro tomorrow.
Ella no trabaja el lunes que viene.	She is not working next Monday.
¿Vienes mañana?	Are you coming tomorrow?
Esta noche cenamos con unos amigos.	We are having dinner with some friends tonight.

When using the simple present to refer to future arrangements or plans, there must always be a reference to the future in the context; otherwise the present tense only refers to the present.

Similarly to English, the simple present of the construction *ir a* + infinitive (applicable also in the preceding examples) can be used when referring to intentions or plans and, in general, to refer to the future (including predictions) when the speaker has some evidence in the present:

Vamos a tener problemas.	We are going to have problems.
Ella no va a venir a la fiesta.	She isn't going to come to the party.
Va a nevar.	It is going to snow.

In predictions, the simple present is possible if the degree of certainty is very high:

Ella no me invita, seguro.	She is not going to invite me, I'm sure.
Mañana lo consigues, seguro.	You are going to get it tomorrow, I'm sure.

The impersonal verb form *hay* (*there is/there are*), which is a variation of the auxiliary verb *haber* (*there . . . be*), remains unchanged when talking about plans or intentions:

Mañana no hay clases.	There are no classes tomorrow.
Esta noche hay un gran partido.	There is a great match tonight.

It can also be used in predictions with a high degree of certainty. If *ir a* is used, it must always be placed before the infinitive *haber*:

Va a haber una reunión.	There is going to be a meeting.
Va a haber problemas.	There are going to be problems.

The auxiliaries placed before *haber* must always be singular. It is not correct to say *Van a haber*.

Exercise 1

Fill in the blanks with the simple present or the present continuous of the verbs in parentheses. Use both tenses where possible.

1. Mañana _____ (yo tener) una reunión muy importante.

2. ¿A qué hora _____ (llegar) el avión?

3. Ana no puede salir ahora. _____ (Ella estudiar).

4. Esta noche _____ (yo no cenar) con mis padres.

5. Los invitados _____ (salir) de la iglesia en este momento.

6. _____ (Pasar) muchas cosas extrañas últimamente.

7. Carlos, ¿qué _____ (tú ir) a hacer con esta tela vieja?

8. Ella _____ (tener que) recoger a Pedro en el aeropuerto el lunes que viene.

Exercise 2

Correct any mistakes.

1. Ellos viven de momento en un apartamento de los padres de ella.

   _____

2. Estos ejercicios me están costando un enorme esfuerzo.

   _____

3. Estoy teniendo que hacer esto para ella. _____

4. Estoy creyendo que estás siendo infantil. _____

5. Estamos yendo a comprar unas cortinas para nuestra habitación.

   _____

6. El sábado hay una fiesta en la casa de Jorge.

   _____

7. ¡Nunca estás hablando conmigo! _____

Exercise 3
Underline the correct option.

1. ¿Te *echo/estoy echando* una mano con esto?

2. La semana que viene me *voy/estoy yendo* de vacaciones.

3. ¡Tú siempre *discutes/estás discutiendo* con Elena!

4. Estoy enfadado, porque nunca *vienes/estás viniendo* a visitarme.

5. No *necesito/estoy necesitando* comprar más comida para la fiesta de mañana.

6. ¿Cuánto *pesa/está pesando* ese cerdo?

7. Nadie me *va/está yendo* a decir lo que *tengo/estoy teniendo* que hacer.

8. *Paso/Estoy pasando* una mala racha con mi hijo.

Exercise 4

Fill in the blanks with the simple present or the present continuous of the verbs that follow.

hablar	ir	tener
comer	trabajar	ganar
oler	alquilar	cerrar

1. Mañana yo no _____ porque el negocio _____ por inventario.

2. Estoy convencido de que mi equipo _____ el campeonato.

3. Antonio _____ varios idiomas. En este momento _____ en alemán con un turista.

4. En este momento la comitiva _____ hacia el salón de actos.

5. ¡Qué bien _____! ¿Qué (nosotros) _____?

6. ¿Qué tal si (nosotros) _____ una película?

7. ¿Es que no ves que (yo) _____ una conversación con este señor?

Exercise 5

Five of the following sentences contain mistakes. Correct them.

1. ¿Qué te parece si estamos cogiendo ese avión?

   _____

2. Te estoy debiendo mucho dinero. _____

3. Creo que el río Guadalquivir está desembocando en el

   Mediterráneo. _____

4. Mañana no estoy almorzando con mis padres.

   _____

5. Estoy teniendo algunos problemas con mi jefe.

   _____

6. Hoy llueve, seguro. _____

7. No vayas ahora, porque arreglan la sala de estar.

   _____

8. Estás siendo muy antipático. _____

Interrogative Sentences and Question Tags

There are some important aspects of interrogative structures that deserve special attention.

Questions in General

As you know, Spanish doesn't need auxiliary verbs to make questions. The subject can be inverted, but this is usually not necessary, especially in casual conversation. In fact, the position of the subject may be anywhere in the sentence when there is no interrogative pronoun:

¿Juan es profesor?	Is Juan a teacher?
¿Es Juan profesor?	
¿Es profesor Juan?	

When subject pronouns are left out, questions have exactly the same structure as affirmative sentences:

¿Eres español?	Are you Spanish?
¿Estáis bien?	Are you (*pl., fam.*) all right?

With the interrogatives *qué* and *cuál*, it is not possible to put the subject between the interrogative and the verb, unless the speaker is choosing or specifying. The sentence *What does Paco do on Saturdays?* can be **¿Qué hace Paco los sábados?**, **¿Qué hace los sábados Paco?**, and **¿Paco qué hace los sábados?**, but the sentence **¿Qué Paco viene los sábados?**

means that there are several people called Paco and the speaker wants to know which one comes on Saturdays.

With other interrogatives, the subject never goes between the interrogative pronoun and the verb, except with **por qué** (*why*), which sometimes admits this position in very emphatic sentences. In some Spanish-speaking areas (Cuba, for example), speakers often place the subject between any interrogative and the verb, e.g., **¿Qué tú vas a comprar?** This is *not* correct.

The interrogative pronoun **quién** can be the subject and the object of the question. When it is the object, it must be preceded by the preposition **a**:

¿Quién tiene las llaves?	Who has the keys?
¿A quién estás llamando?	Whom are you phoning?

When the verb sequence consists of more than one verb, the position of the subject may go anywhere (with the exceptions previously made):

¿Va a estar trabajando Luis?	Is Luis going to be working?
¿Va a estar Luis trabajando?	
¿Luis va a estar trabajando?	
¿Va Luis a estar trabajando?	

But it is not possible to put the subject between the verb **haber** (in perfect tenses) and the past participle. **¿Has tú comido?** is incorrect.

Question Tags

As Spanish doesn't use auxiliaries in questions and negatives, *question tags* simply consist of the word **no** (even after affirmative sentences) or **verdad** (*true*) at the end of the sentence:

Tú eres Pedro, ¿no/verdad?	You are Pedro, aren't you?
Ella no fuma, ¿no/verdad?	She doesn't smoke, does she?

There are no exact question tags after imperatives or *let's* structures:

Dame eso, ¿quieres?	Give me that, will you?
Siéntate, ¿quieres?	Sit down, will you?

Alárgame el martillo, ¿puedes?	Hand me the hammer, will you?
Comamos aquí, ¿vale/de acuerdo?	Let's eat here, shall we?

As you can see, the verb **querer** can follow imperatives, but if the speaker considers that the person spoken to could have difficulty in doing the action, **poder** can be used instead.

Depending on the speaker's attitude (insisting or irritated), **no**, **vale**, and **de acuerdo** can be used after imperatives:

Come con nosotros, ¿no?	Eat with us, will you?
Cállate, ¿vale?	Be quiet, will you?

Vale and **de acuerdo** are also used when the speaker is making a decision or offering to do something:

Yo te ayudo con los deberes, ¿vale?	I'll help you with your homework, OK?
Yo traigo las bebidas, ¿de acuerdo?	I'll bring the drinks, all right?

If the speaker is not making a decision or offering to do something, **no** must be used.

Exercise 1

Make up questions for the following answers. Use the underlined words as a cue as in the example.

Carlos tiene <u>dos</u> niños.
¿Cuántos niños tiene Carlos?

1. Hay <u>galletas</u>.

_____

2. Sara va a visitar <u>Canadá</u> este año.

_____

3. Los hermanos de Antonio estudian <u>arquitectura</u>.

_____

4. Elena es <u>alta, rubia y muy bonita</u>.

_____

5. Ella suele ir al colegio <u>en bicicleta</u>.

_____

6. <u>Pablo</u> vive en esa casa.

_____

7. Esta lámpara cuesta <u>treinta dólares</u>.

_____

8. Voy a invitar a <u>todos mis amigos</u>.

_____

9. Mañana tengo que empezar <u>a las siete</u>.

_____

10. No quiero comer <u>nada</u>, gracias.

_____

Exercise 2

Finish the following sentences with a question tag.

1. Ella ya tiene dos niños, ¿_____?

2. Préstame un poco de dinero, ¿_____?

3. ¡Para ya de hacer ruido! ¿_____?

4. Te recojo a las seis, ¿_____? (*offer*)

5. Va a haber un gran lío con todo esto, ¿_____?

Confusing Verbs, Part 1

This and the following chapters on confusing verbs cover a selection of verbs that either have a very wide semantic range or offer special difficulties in their usage.

Tener que

Tener que means *to have to* when talking about obligation:

Yo tengo que estudiar.	I have to study.
Ella tiene que trabajar.	She has to work.

As in English, **no tener que** expresses lack of obligation to do something:

No tengo que trabajar mañana.	I don't have to work tomorrow.
Ella no tiene que hacer el examen.	She doesn't have to take the exam.

With **usted/ustedes**, inversion is very frequent:

Tiene usted que rellenar este formulario.	You have to fill out this form.
Tienen ustedes que pasar la aduana.	You have to go through customs.

No tener por qué is often used instead of **no tener que**. They are entirely equivalent in many cases, but **no tener por qué** normally conveys the idea of free choice. The sentence **No tengo que trabajar**

37

mañana means that I have the day off tomorrow, but the sentence **No tengo por qué trabajar mañana** implies that I can choose not to go to work. **No tener que** expresses lack of obligation to do something, maybe imposed by a timetable, the boss, etc. **No tener por qué** expresses that the speaker is free to choose.

Llevar

Llevar puesto (*to wear, to have on*) is highly unusual in the continuous, or progressive, tense. This verb refers to items of clothing, shoes, hats, glasses, etc., but it cannot refer to a moustache, a beard, a tattoo, etc. **Puesto** is an adjective that has to show agreement of gender and number with the accompanying noun:

Ella lleva puesta una falda roja.	She is wearing a red skirt.
Ella lleva una falda roja puesta.	
Él lleva puestos unos zapatos.	He is wearing shoes.

The adjective **puesto** can be left out. When this is the case, the verb **llevar** can be used to refer to a tattoo, a moustache, etc. and is translated as *to have*:

Ella lleva una blusa azul.	She is wearing a blue blouse.
Él lleva bigote.	He has a moustache.

The verb **llevar** can also mean *to take somebody/something somewhere*:

Voy a llevar a mi hijo al cine.	I'm going to take my son to the movies.
No puedo llevarte al aeropuerto.	I can't take you to the airport.

The verb **llevar** is also used to mean *to carry*:

Ella no puede llevar las bolsas.	She can't carry the bags.
Él lleva dos cajas.	He is carrying two boxes.

Continuous tenses with **llevar** are possible, except when it means *to wear*, but are not usual.

Coger/Recoger

The verb ***coger*** (*to take, to catch*) is a spelling-changing verb. It changes the **g** to **j** in some of its forms to maintain the same pronunciation of the **g** in the infinitive. The letter **g** before **e** and **i** is a strong guttural sound like a strongly aspirated English *h*, but before **a**, **o**, and **u** it becomes a soft sound like the *g* in the English verb *give*. The simple present of ***coger*** is:

yo cojo
tú coges
él/ella/Ud. coge
nosotros cogemos
vosotros cogéis
ellos/ellas/Uds. cogen

Ellos cogieron el tren.	They took the train.
La niña está cogiendo las galletas.	The girl is taking the cookies.
¡Coge el balón!	Catch the ball!
Cogí un resfriado.	I caught a cold.

The verb ***coger*** can't be used to mean *to take somebody/something somewhere.*

Coger is also used to mean *to pick up/answer* (the phone):

Yo no quiero coger el teléfono.	I don't want to pick up/answer the phone.

Recoger is used instead of ***coger*** to mean *to pick up* in the sense of *picking up or collecting people or things after having taken them to a certain place* (clothes from the laundry, children from school, etc.):

Fui al colegio a recoger a mis niños.	I went to the school to pick up my children.

Recoger (not ***coger***) implies *putting things away*:

Tienes que recoger esos juguetes.	You have to put away those toys.

Both **coger** and **recoger** can be used to *pick* something *up* from the floor:

Coge/Recoge eso del suelo.   Pick that up from the floor.

Both **coger** and **recoger** can be used in agricultural contexts, but **recoger** is more common in Latin America:

Tenemos que recoger la fruta.   We have to pick the fruit.

When in doubt, just think that **recoger** is connected with the idea of returning.

In some Latin American regions (Argentina, for example), **coger** has sexual nuances. Speakers in these regions avoid the word and in its place use **pillar**, **agarrar**, or **tomar**.

Enseñar

Enseñar has two meanings in English: *to teach* and *to show*:

Ella me enseñó inglés.   She taught me English.
Les enseñé mi casa.   I showed them my house.

Apagar

Apagar means *to turn off, switch off,* and *put out*:

Tienes que apagar la radio.   You have to turn off the radio.
Ellos no pueden apagar el fuego.   They can't put out the fire.

In some Spanish-speaking areas, especially in Spain, **quitar** and **apagar** are interchangeable when they refer to radio and TV:

Tienes que apagar/quitar la tele.   You have to turn off the TV.

Escuchar/Mirar

Escuchar and **mirar**, among many other verbs, are followed by the preposition **a** when they refer to people:

Estoy mirando los coches.	I'm looking at the cars.
Estoy mirando a tu hermana.	I'm looking at your sister.
¿Qué estás escuchando?	What are you listening to?
¿A quién estás escuchando?	Who are you listening to?

Hacer

The irregular verb ***hacer*** usually translates as *to do* and *to make*:

hacer la cama	to make the bed
hacer un pastel	to make a cake
hacer amigos	to make friends
hacer un esfuerzo	to make an effort
hacer un favor	to do a favor

In the construction *to make a speech* (***dar un discurso***), the verb ***dar*** (*to give*) is used more often:

Ella está dando un discurso.	She is making a speech.

The English construction *do the + -ing* has some equivalent constructions in Spanish (verb + ***la*** + noun):

hacer la comida	to do the cooking
hacer la compra	to do the shopping
hacer la colada	to do the washing

Lavar la ropa is more common than ***hacer la colada***.

To do the dishes and *to do the ironing* translate as **lavar los platos** and **planchar**. *To do the cleaning* can be translated as ***hacer la limpieza***, but **limpiar** is much more common:

Ella está lavando los platos.	She is doing/washing the dishes.
Hoy no puedo planchar.	Today I can't do the ironing.
Tengo que limpiar.	I have to do the cleaning.

Encender

Encender can be translated as *to turn on, to switch on,* and *to light.* It is a stem-changing verb (**e** to **ie**):

No quiero encender la televisión.   I don't want to turn on the TV.
Él no puede encender un cigarrillo.   He can't light a cigarette.

In some Spanish-speaking areas, especially in Spain, **poner** and **encender** are interchangeable when they refer to radio and TV:

No quiero encender/poner la tele.   I don't want to turn on the TV.

Exercise 1

Fill in the blanks with the present tense, the gerund, or the infinitive of the verbs that follow. Some verbs can be used more than once.

coger (pillar)	apagar	dar
enseñar	recoger	hacer
encender	llevar	

1. A las siete tengo que _____ a los niños de la clase de música.

2. Tengo que _____ la comida.

3. La chica que _____ la blusa azul es mi hermana.

4. ¿No puedes _____ ese puro? ¡El humo me molesta!

5. Mañana tengo que _____ un discurso en la universidad.

6. Este coche pierde aceite. Lo tengo que _____ al taller.

7. Vas a _____ un resfriado.

8. Te voy a _____ mi casa.

9. Te voy a _____ a mi casa.

10. ¿Por qué no _____ (tú) todo lo que está en el suelo?

Exercise 2
Fill in the blanks with the present tense of *ir a* or ***tener que***.

1. Esta habitación está muy sucia. (Tú) _____ limpiarla.

2. Carla dice que no _____ casarse con ese hombre.

3. Paco _____ perder peso. Está engordando mucho.

4. ¿(Yo) _____ pagar ahora, o puedo hacerlo la semana que viene?

5. Ese es el coche que _____ comprar los padres de Tomás.

6. El banco dice que nosotros no _____ poder obtener el segundo préstamo.

7. Ya sabes que _____ hacer tus tareas antes de jugar con tus amigos.

Exercise 3
Fill in the blanks with the present tense of ***no tener que*** or ***no tener por qué***.

1. La semana que viene es Navidad y (nosotros)

    _____ trabajar.

2. El profesor nos ha dicho que (nosotros) _____
hacer el último ejercicio.

3. ¡(Yo) _____ aguantar esto! ¡Me marcho!

4. (Tú) _____ cocinar mañana. Podemos ir a un
restaurante.

5. (Tú) _____ cocinar mañana, ya que vamos a ir a
un restaurante.

6. Yo _____ ir a la oficina todos los días. Soy el jefe.

7. Cada uno puede llevar puesto lo que quiera, así que (tú)
_____ ponerte una corbata.

Reflexive Pronouns and Reflexive Verbs

Reflexive pronouns play a very important role in Spanish tense construction, as they are used not only to refer to actual reflexive actions but also to indicate that the action refers to the subject of the sentence in nonreflexive situations. Their use determines the exact meaning of the sentence.

Reflexive Pronouns
The Spanish reflexive pronouns are:

me	myself
te	yourself (sing., fam.)
se	himself/herself/itself/yourself (sing., form.)
nos	ourselves
os	yourselves (pl., fam.)
se	yourselves (pl., form.), themselves

Remember that ***usted*** and ***ustedes*** always require third-person forms (***se***).

These pronouns are used with transitive reflexive verbs when the subject and the object of the sentence are the same. Compare:

	direct object
Él lava la ropa.	He washes the clothes.
	direct object
Él se lava.	He washes himself. (reflexive action)

Reflexive pronouns are always placed before the first verb, but if there is a gerund or an infinitive in the verb sequence, they can also be placed after the gerund and after the infinitive:

Yo me divierto.	I enjoy myself.
Tú te diviertes.	You (sing., fam.) enjoy yourself.
Ella se divierte.	She enjoys herself.
Usted se divierte.	You (sing., form.) enjoy yourself.
Nosotros nos divertimos.	We enjoy ourselves.
Vosotros os divertís.	You (pl., fam.) enjoy yourselves.
Yo me estoy divirtiendo.	I am enjoying myself.
Yo estoy divirtiéndome.	
Yo me quiero divertir.	I want to enjoy myself.
Yo quiero divertirme.	

The irregular verb **divertir(se)** changes the **e** in the stem to **ie**. The gerund is **divirtiendo** and the stress falls on the diphthong **ie**. Even if an extra syllable is added to this gerund (when a reflexive pronoun is attached to it), it retains the stress on the **ie** by means of a written accent: **divirtiéndose**.

Reflexive Verbs

Spanish uses reflexive pronouns with all types of verbs, transitive and intransitive, true reflexive or not, as long as the action refers in any way to the subject:

Ella no se siente muy bien.	She doesn't feel very well.
Él no se quiere sentar.	He doesn't want to sit down.
Yo me quiero quedar aquí.	I want to stay here.

This habit of using reflexive pronouns with many verbs occurs even in sentences where there is a clear direct object:

Me voy a comprar un coche.	I'm going to buy a car (for myself).
Ella no se quiere comer la manzana.	She doesn't want to eat the apple.

Many verbs can be used without reflexive pronouns. ***Voy a pedir una pizza*** *(I'm going to order a pizza)* is correct, but **<u>Me</u> voy a pedir una pizza** makes it very clear who the pizza is for. ***Ella no quiere marchar*** doesn't sound as Spanish as ***Ella no <u>se</u> quiere marchar*** *(She doesn't want to leave)*. The following examples will make this clear:

Yo siento el brazo del niño.   I can feel the child's arm.

But if I want to talk about my own health or feelings, I will have to say ***Yo <u>me</u> siento bien.*** *(I feel well.)*

Yo siento a mi hijo.   I make my son sit down.

Here, the verb ***sentar*** means *to make somebody sit down*, but if I want to sit down myself, I must say ***Yo <u>me</u> siento*** (the irregular verb ***sentarse*** means *to sit down*). To show that a verb is reflexive, the pronoun ***se*** is added to the infinitive. The verbs ***sentar*** and ***sentir*** have the same first-person conjugation in the present.

If a mother is washing her child's hair, she says ***<u>Le</u> estoy lavando el pelo a mi hijo*** *(I'm washing my child's hair)*, but if she is washing her own hair, she says ***<u>Me</u> estoy lavando el pelo*** *(I'm washing my hair)*. Note that English uses possessive adjectives *(my hair)*; Spanish uses definite articles *(**el pelo**)*.

With certain verbs, the use of reflexive pronouns expresses nuances that have something to do with the action being definitive or not. The verb ***ir*** *(to go)* is a good example. If I am at a party and I want to leave, I say ***Me voy*** *(I'm going/I'm leaving)*, or if I am at work and I want to say that I'm going home (to stay there), I say ***Me voy a mi casa*** *(I'm going home)*. But if I bump into a friend in the middle of the street and he asks me where I am going, I say ***Voy a mi casa. Me voy...*** is a definitive action (a decision to leave); ***Voy...*** only expresses that I am on my way.

Another good example is the verb ***comer*** *(to eat)*. The use of reflexive pronouns with this verb often implies the idea of completion, especially with an article. In English, this idea of completion with verbs like *eat* and *drink* is expressed with the word *up*:

Él siempre se come las galletas.   He always eats up the cookies.

Él siempre se come galletas is not acceptable because the reflexive pronoun requires the use of an article.

Él siempre come galletas.	He always eats cookies. (*just a habit*)

Here are some more examples:

Yo estoy tocando el tejido.	I am touching the cloth.
Yo me estoy tocando la nariz.	I am touching my nose.
Tienes que acostar a los niños.	You have to put the children to bed.
Tienes que acostarte.	You have to go to bed.
Ella viene a mi casa mañana.	She is coming to my house tomorrow.
Ella se viene a mi casa mañana.	She is coming to my house tomorrow. (*She is coming to stay with me for some time.*)
Ellos vienen de Argentina.	They come from Argentina. (*origin*)
Ellos <u>se</u> vienen de Argentina.	They are coming from Argentina. (*This sentence implies that they are coming from Argentina to stay here for some time; it can be forever or just for a vacation.*)
Estoy bebiendo leche.	I am drinking milk.
Me estoy bebiendo la leche.	I am drinking (up) my milk. (*Remember: Reflexive pronouns require the presence of articles.*)

As you can see from these examples, many Spanish verbs have a different meaning when they are used with reflexive pronouns:

Yo siempre pongo esto allí.	I always put this there.
Yo siempre me pongo una bufanda.	I always put on a scarf.
Ella acuesta a los niños a las ocho.	She puts her children to bed at eight.

Ella se acuesta muy tarde.	She goes to bed very late.
Yo llamo a mis niños.	I call my children.
Yo me llamo Pedro.	My name is Pedro.

The verb ***llamar*** (*to name*) is used with reflexive pronouns to talk about the names of people, animals, and things:

Yo me llamo Antonio.	My name is Antonio.
Tú te llamas Carlos.	Your name is Carlos.
Ella se llama María.	Her name is María.

Mi nombre es Antonio, **Tu nombre es Carlos**, and **Su nombre es María** are all correct, but the verb ***llamarse*** is more common, especially in questions:

| *¿Cómo te llamas?* | What is your name? |

Reflexive pronouns can appear together with object pronouns in the same sentence, but the reflexive pronouns must always be placed before the object pronouns:

| *Yo me lo estoy poniendo.* | I am putting it on. |
| *Yo estoy poniéndomelo.* | I am putting it on. |

Verbs Like *Gustar*

There is an important category of verbs that express liking, disliking, accepting, etc. The most common ones are:

gustar	to like
disgustar	to dislike
encantar	to love
apetecer	to feel like
importar	to mind
parecer	to seem

These verbs pose an additional problem: they aren't usually conjugated with subject pronouns, but rather with a combination of object pronouns (*a mí me*, *a ti te*, *a él/ella le*, etc). In addition, they are usually used only in their third-person forms:

(a mí) me gusta	I like
(Not: *gusto*)	
(a ti) te gusta	you (sing., fam.) like
(a él/ella/Ud.) le gusta	he/she likes; you (sing., form.) like
(a nosotros) nos gusta	we like
(a vosotros) os gusta	you (pl., fam.) like
(a Uds./ellos) les gusta	you (pl., form.)/they like

The words in parentheses can be omitted if the speaker considers the context clear enough:

Me gusta el vino.	I like wine.
A ella no le gusta la cerveza.	She doesn't like beer.

The word preceded by the preposition *a* can also be a noun:

A Juan le encanta el marisco.	Juan loves seafood.
A María no le gusta esta casa.	María doesn't like this house.

If the object is plural, the verb is conjugated in its third-person plural form:

Me gusta el pescado.	I like fish.
Me gustan las manzanas.	I like apples.

It is possible to mention the object first:

El pescado me encanta.	I love fish.
El café no le gusta a mi marido.	My husband doesn't like coffee.

These verbs can be followed by infinitives. When this is the case, they never admit plural forms:

Me gusta bailar.	I like dancing.
A ella no le gusta leer libros.	She doesn't like reading books.

No me importa esperar.	I don't mind waiting.
¿Te apetece tomar un café?	Do you feel like having a coffee?

The words preceded by the preposition *a* admit several positions in questions:

¿A ti te gusta el té?	Do you like tea?
¿Te gusta a ti el té?	
¿Te gusta el té a ti?	

When these verbs refer to the subject, they follow a normal conjugation with subject pronouns. **Yo gusto** means that *I am liked (by people).* If I need to say who I am liked by, I will have to put the object pronoun before the verb: **Yo le gusto a tu madre** (*Your mother likes me*). The construction order in English is the opposite:

Tú me gustas (a mí).	I like you.
Yo te gusto.	You like me.
Tú no le gustas a mi madre.	My mother doesn't like you.
Ella no les gusta a mis padres.	My parents don't like her.

The words before *a* can appear in several positions:

Ella no les gusta a ellos.	They don't like her.
Ella a ellos no les gusta.	
A ellos ella no les gusta.	

Inversion of the subject is possible:

A ti no te gusto yo.	You don't like me.

Note that these verbs have a "normal" conjugation when they refer to first- and second-person direct objects:

A ella le gusta el pueblo.	She likes the town.
A ella le gustas tú.	She likes you.
A usted le gusta este país.	You like this country.
A usted no le gustamos nosotros.	You don't like us.

Remember that **usted** and **ustedes** always go with third-person forms (**le** and **les** in this type of conjugation).

A big difference with English is that verbs like **gustar**, **encantar**, etc., can be used in the progressive form. A sentence like **Me está gustando la fiesta** means that *I like what I have seen so far*.

These verbs and this type of conjugation must not be confused with sentences in Spanish that have indirect objects that are represented by an object pronoun such as **le** and **a** + noun or subject pronoun (**a Juan, a él**):

Yo le voy a dar a Juan ese regalo.	I am going to give Juan that present.
Ella le va a leer el libro a él.	She is going to read the book to him.

This occurs with the direct object too, but only with pronouns, never with nouns, unless the noun appears as a direct object at the beginning of the sentence:

No voy a llamar a María.	I am not going to phone María.
<u>*A María* no *la* voy a llamar.</u>	

In sentences where the direct object is represented by an object pronoun, third-person pronouns in the function of *indirect* object are all replaced by **se**:

Se lo voy a dar (a ellos).	I am going to give it to them.

Get + Adjective/Past Participle

Many English constructions with *get* + adjective or past participle use reflexive verbs in Spanish:

casarse	to get married
cansarse	to get tired
emborracharse	to get drunk
aburrirse	to get bored

prepararse	to get ready
acostumbrarse	to get used to

Ella se casa la semana que viene.	She is getting married next week.
(Yo) Me estoy aburriendo.	I'm getting bored.
Tenemos que prepararnos.	We have to get ready.
(Tú) Te vas a emborrachar.	You are going to get drunk.

Some English expressions with *get* are translated by the irregular verb **poner** (*to put*) + reflexive pronoun + adjective or adverb:

ponerse enfermo	to get sick
ponerse difícil	to get difficult
ponerse mejor	to get better
ponerse nervioso	to get nervous

Ella se pone enferma todos los veranos.	She gets sick every summer.
(Yo) Me estoy poniendo nervioso.	I am getting nervous.
La vida se está poniendo muy difícil.	Life is getting very difficult.

Ponerse may also be translated as ***to become*** in the preceding examples.

Other expressions in English with *get* use the verbs ***dar*** (*to give*) and ***entrar*** (*to enter*) with a noun. The first person of the irregular verb ***dar*** is ***yo doy***; the rest follows a regular pattern. The verb ***entrar*** is regular. With the nouns ***hambre*** (*hunger*), ***sed*** (*thirst*), ***calor*** (*heat*), and **frío** (*cold*), these verbs are conjugated like the verb ***gustar***:

entrar/dar hambre	to get hungry
entrar/dar sed	to get thirsty
entrar/dar frío	to get cold
entrar/dar calor	to get hot

(A mí) Me está dando hambre.	I am getting hungry.
A ella le está dando sed.	She is getting thirsty.

A ellos les está dando frío.	They are getting cold.
Me está dando calor.	I am getting hot.

When the speaker refers to the temperature of objects, food, liquid, etc., *to get hot* translates as **calentarse** (irregular), and *to get cold* translates as **enfriarse** (regular, with stress variations):

Este cable se está calentando.	This wire is getting hot.
La leche se está enfriando.	The milk is getting cold.

In talking about temperature increase or decrease in a certain place, Spanish uses the construction **empezar a** + **hacer** + noun:

Está empezando a hacer calor.	It's getting hot.
Está empezando a hacer frío.	It's getting cold.

In this construction, the verb **empezar** (*to begin*) is conjugated without a subject because it acts as an impersonal verb in such cases.

In questions with gerunds and infinitives, the subject may appear in any position:

¿A usted le está dando frío?	Are you getting cold?
¿Le está dando frío a usted?	
¿Le está a usted dando frío?	
¿Le está dando a usted frío?	

As you know, when the context is clear, the subject can be omitted: *¿Le está dando frío?*

To get/become late translates as **hacerse tarde**, and *to get dark* translates as **oscurecer** (irregular and without reflexive pronouns). These verbs are always conjugated without a subject because they are impersonal verbs:

Se está haciendo tarde.	It's getting late.
Está oscureciendo.	It's getting dark.

Reciprocal Actions (*Each Other/One Another*)

In talking about actions with a reciprocal effect (things done to *each other* or *one another*), reflexive pronouns are also used:

Ellos no se hablan.	They don't talk to each other.
Luis y Juan se odian.	Luis and Juan hate each other.
Los vecinos se ven todos los días.	The neighbors see each other every day.

The phrase **llevarse bien/mal (con)** means *to get on well/badly (with)*. When the subjects referred to appear before the verbs, prepositions are not needed; but when one of the subjects comes after the verb (it then becomes a complement), the preposition is necessary. Compare:

Nosotros nos llevamos muy bien.	We get along very well (with each other).
Yo me llevo muy bien con mi mujer.	I get along very well with my wife.

The verb **hablar** and other verbs that require the preposition **con** can be used in the same way, but verbs that require a different preposition cannot:

Carlos y Rogelio no <u>se</u> hablan.	Carlos and Rogelio don't talk to each other.
Carlos no <u>se</u> habla <u>con</u> Rogelio.	Carlos doesn't talk to Rogelio.
Ellos <u>se</u> aman.	They love each other.
(Not: *Ella <u>se</u> ama <u>a</u> su marido.*)	

Combination of *Se* and Object Pronouns

The reflexive pronoun **se** must be followed by the object pronouns (**me**, **te**, **le**, **nos**, **os**, **les**) used in the conjugation of the verb **gustar** to indicate who the action refers to. The sentence **El coche se averió** (*The car broke down*) doesn't say who suffered the consequences of the breakdown, but the sentence **El coche <u>se me</u> averió** clearly indicates that it was my car or the car that I was driving at that moment. Here are some more examples:

A ella se le va a caer el sombrero.	Her hat is going to fall off.
El ladrón se nos escapó (a nosotros).	The thief escaped (from) us.
Se me está acabando el tiempo (a mí).	I'm running out of time.

The order in these sentences can be inverted (***El sombrero se le va a caer***, ***Se nos escapó el ladrón***, ***El dinero se me está acabando***). The words following *a* (*a mí*, *a ella*, etc.) are used for emphasis or to clarify the context.

When using ***se*** and object pronouns, possessives are not common. A sentence like ***El dinero se me está acabando*** is preferable to ***Mi dinero se me está acabando.***

Some verbs can leave out the object pronoun without changing the meaning:

Juan <u>se</u> rompió un brazo.	Juan broke an arm.
A Juan <u>se le</u> rompió un brazo.	

With other verbs there are certain nuances:

Ella perdió el dinero.	She lost her/the money. (*maybe by accident or by making a bad investment, etc.*)
A ella <u>se le</u> perdió el dinero.	She lost her money. (*only by accident*)

Se takes the place of the direct object pronouns ***lo***, ***la***, ***los***, and ***las***. Compare:

Ella lo perdió.	She lost it.
A ella se le perdió.	She lost it.
(Never: *A ella se le lo perdió.*)	

Exercise 1

Put the verbs in parentheses into the present, present continuous, or infinitive. Use reflexive and/or object pronouns where necessary.

1. Los Suárez _____ (marchar) de vacaciones en julio.

2. Yo no quiero _____ (sentar) al lado de la ventana.

3. Ella dice que nosotros no podemos _____ (quedar) hasta tan tarde.

4. ¿Por qué (tú) no _____ (acostar) a los niños mientras yo

   _____ (duchar)?

5. ¿Usted _____ (sentir) bien?

6. Ella va a _____ (montar) en un taxi.

7. No debes _____ (montar) a desconocidos en el coche.

8. A Jaime _____ (encantar) pescar con su padre.

Exercise 2

Correct any mistakes.

1. Ella se niega los hechos. _____

2. Ella niega a ir a esa boda. _____

3. No puedes arriesgar todo tu dinero. _____

4. No debes arriesgarte a ser detenido. _____

5. A su hija le puede torcer el tobillo otra vez. _____

6. Mi hermana y su novio siempre dicen palabras de amor el uno al

   otro. _____

7. A mis padres no les puedo decir nada de esto.

   _____

8. A mi hermano no se importa que usemos su moto.

   _____

Exercise 3

Change the following sentences as in the example.

Nuestra gasolina se está acabando.
Se nos está acabando la gasolina.

1. Tu camisa se está arrugando.

   _____

2. El pelo de Pedro se está cayendo.

   _____

3. Las cosas de Luisa se están poniendo muy difíciles.

   _____

4. Tú no puedes olvidar mi cumpleaños.

   _____

5. Tu cara se está poniendo roja.

   _____

Confusing Verbs, Part 2

Pasar/Ocurrir

Both **pasar** and **ocurrir** mean *to happen* and *to happen to somebody/something*. As such, they are conjugated in the third person singular and plural forms, like the verb **gustar**:

Algo está pasando/ocurriendo.	Something is happening.
¿Qué pasa/ocurre?	What is happening?
¿Qué está pasando/ocurriendo?	
¿Qué pasa/ocurre si abro la puerta?	What happens if I open the door?
A ella le pasan/ocurren cosas extrañas.	Strange things happen to her.
Eso no me puede pasar/ocurrir a mí.	That can't happen to me.

Both verbs can also mean *to be the matter (with)* and *to be wrong (with)*:

¿Qué pasa/ocurre?	What's the matter?/What's wrong?
¿Qué te pasa/ocurre?	What's wrong with you?
¿Qué le pasa a tu coche?	What's wrong with your car?
A ella le pasa/ocurre algo.	There's something wrong with her./Something is happening to her.

Pasar (but not *ocurrir*) can also mean *to spend time*:

Yo siempre paso las Navidades con ellos.	I always spend Christmas with them.
Ella va a pasar unos días conmigo.	She is going to spend a few days with me.

In the following sentences reflexive pronouns are added to emphasize the fact that the action happens too often, or that the duration of the action is too long:

Ella se pasa el día comiendo.	She eats all day long. (*Literally:* She spends her day eating.)
Me paso la vida trabajando.	I work too much. (*Literally:* I spend my life working.)

Pasar (without reflexive pronouns) is also used to mean *to go by, to pass by, to pass, to get in*:

El tiempo pasa muy deprisa.	Time goes by very fast.
Puedes pasar.	You can come in.
¿Me puedes pasar la sal?	Can you pass me the salt?

In general, the verb *pasar* can refer to any kind of movement (physical or imaginary) from one place to another:

Ella no nos quiere pasar a la cocina.	She doesn't want to show us into the kitchen.
Debes pasar esto al español.	You must translate this into Spanish.
Tienes que pasar esto a la otra mesa.	You have to put this on the other table. (*Now it is on this table, but it must be put on the other one.*)

Pasar can be used with reflexive pronouns when the action of moving from place to place refers to the subject:

Debes pasarte a la otra habitación.	You must go to the other room.

Pasarse also means *to call on*. With this meaning, the preposition **por** is used:

El médico se pasó por nuestra casa.   The doctor called on us/our house.

Pasar can even be used as an informal greeting:

Hola, Antonio, ¿qué pasa?   Hello, Antonio, how's life?

Encantar

The verb **encantar** can't be used to express romantic love. In this case, the regular verb **amar** is used, although many people prefer the stem-changing (*e* to *ie*) verb **querer**:

Yo te amo/quiero.   I love you.

Marchar

The reflexive verb **marcharse** means *to leave for a place*. It can be used with the prepositions **a** and **para**:

Mañana me marcho a/para Londres.   I'm leaving for London tomorrow.

Dejar/Abandonar/Parar

The verb **dejar** has several meanings:

No puedo dejar mi coche aquí.	I can't leave my car here.
Él quiere dejar a su mujer.	He wants to leave his wife (forever).
Ella no nos deja ver al bebé.	She doesn't let us see the baby.
Ella no me quiere dejar su libro.	She doesn't want to lend me her book.

The verb **abandonar** usually means *to leave someone/something forever*:

Él abandonó a sus hijos.   He left his children.

Another frequent meaning of *dejar* is *to give up*. When another verb follows, use the preposition *de*:

No puedo dejar de fumar.	I can't give up (stop) smoking.
No puedo dejarlo.	I can't give it up (smoking).

Parar (*to stop*) and the preposition *de* can also be used with this meaning:

No puedo parar de fumar.	I can't stop smoking.

With pronouns, the verb *parar* is not equivalent to *to give up*. It usually means *to stop something*:

No puedo pararlo.	I can't stop it. (*if* **lo** *refers to a car*)

Preparar

Preparar means *to prepare/make ready*. The verb **prepararse** means *to get ready*:

Estoy preparando el almuerzo.	I am preparing lunch.
Me estoy preparando.	I am getting ready.

Poner

The verb **poner** means *to put*, and the reflexive verb **ponerse** means *to put on*:

Voy a poner esto en esa mesa.	I'm going to put this on that table.
Voy a ponerme los zapatos.	I'm going to put on my shoes.

When the meaning is *to turn on/switch on* (TV and radio), only **poner** is possible:

No quiero poner la tele.	I don't want to turn on the TV.

The verb ***ponerse*** is often used to refer to the place the subject occupies, without specifying if the subject is sitting, standing, or lying down:

Ella siempre se pone a mi derecha.	She always seats herself to my right.
Yo nunca me pongo a la izquierda en la cama.	I never lie on the left side in bed.

Ponerse means *to start an activity* when it is followed by the preposition *a* and an infinitive:

Me puse a limpiar la habitación.	I started to clean the room.

Poner (without reflexive pronouns) can mean *to make somebody do something* or *to get somebody to do something*:

Tienes que ponerles a trabajar.	You have to make them work.

Ponerse also translates some *get* + adjective combinations in English:

Juan se puso muy nervioso.	Juan got very nervous.

Ponerse de pie (*to stand up*) can also be used with the preposition ***en*** (***ponerse en pie***). The reflexive verb ***levantarse*** can also have the same meaning as ***ponerse de pie***.

Exercise 1

Fill in the blanks with the verbs that follow in the present, present continuous, gerund, or infinitive. Some verbs can be used more than once. Add reflexive pronouns where needed.

llorar	dejar	marchar
preparar	abandonar	parar
pasar	poner	

1. Es muy tarde y aún tengo que _____ la cena.

2. Este grifo no _____ de gotear.

3. No debes _____ la puerta abierta.

4. ¿Qué _____, María? ¿Por qué _____?

5. Tienes que _____ para tu actuación.

6. No tienes por qué _____ de pie.

7. Por qué (tú) no _____ por mi casa y tomamos algo?

8. No puedes _____ un coche en mitad de la carretera.

9. Algo grave _____ en casa de los vecinos.

10. Nosotros tenemos que _____. Es ya muy tarde.

Exercise 2
Correct any mistakes.

1. Marta siempre pone muy nerviosa cuando me saluda. _____

2. No puedes abandonar tu bicicleta aquí mientras haces las compras. _____

3. ¿Por qué no te pones a hacer los deberes? _____

4. Cuando entre el presidente, debes poner de pie. _____

5. Mañana me marcho para pasar unos días con mis abuelos.

_____

To Have and *to Be*

There are many cases in which English uses *to be* while Spanish uses *to have*, and there are cases in which the English verbs *to have* and *to take* are translated by different verbs that depend on the action and the situation.

To Have and *to Take*

As you know, *to have* is the irregular verb **tener**, and *to take* is the regular verb **tomar**: **Tengo dos coches** (*I have two cars*), **Tomo el autobús** (*I take the bus*). There are, however, many cases in which *to have* and *to take* are translated by different verbs. The most common ones are:

desayunar	to have breakfast
almorzar	to have lunch
cenar	to have dinner/supper
tomar	to have (*food/drink*)
ducharse	to take a shower
bañarse	to take a bath/swim
pasear	to take a walk

Yo siempre almuerzo a las 12.30.	I always have lunch at 12:30.
Ella desayuna café y tostadas.	She has coffee and toast for breakfast.
Ellos están tomando café.	They are having some coffee.
¿Qué va usted a tomar?	What are you going to have?
Ella se está duchando.	She is taking a shower.
Me voy a bañar.	I'm going to take a bath/swim.
Los niños están paseando.	The children are taking a walk.

The verbs **tomar** and **pasear** may sometimes be used with reflexive pronouns:

Me voy a tomar un café.	I'm going to have a coffee.
Ella se está paseando.	She is taking a walk.

To have breakfast, to have lunch, and *to have dinner* can also be translated as **tomar el desayuno**, **tomar el almuerzo**, and **tomar la cena**. Reflexive pronouns may be added, but these constructions are much less common than **desayunar**, **almorzar**, and **cenar**:

Yo siempre tomo el desayuno en la cocina.	I always have breakfast in the kitchen.
Yo nunca tomo el almuerzo en casa.	I never have lunch at home.
¿A qué hora van ustedes a tomar la cena?	What time are you going to have dinner?

El desayuno, **el almuerzo**, and **la cena** are nouns meaning *breakfast,* *lunch,* and *dinner.* If the food is mentioned, the preposition **de** is used before the name of the meal (**por** is also possible):

Ellos van a tomar pizza de cena.	They are going to have pizza for dinner.

However, **Ellos van a cenar pizza** is much more common.

Instead of **ducharse**, the construction **dar** (*to give*) + reflexive pronoun + **una ducha** can be used. The same applies to **bañarse**: **dar** + reflexive pronoun + **un baño**. Remember that **la ducha** (*shower*) and **el baño** (*bath/swim*) are nouns:

Él se está dando una ducha.	He is taking a shower.
La niña quiere darse un baño.	The girl wants to have a bath/swim.

The same type of construction can be used to translate *to take a walk.* In this case, reflexive pronouns are optional:

Voy a dar(me) un paseo.	I'm going to take a walk.

The verbs *duchar*, *bañar*, and *pasear* are transitive verbs which can take a direct object:

Ella está bañando al bebé.	She is bathing the baby.
Les voy a pasear.	I'm going to take them for a walk.

You can also say ***Les voy a dar un paseo.***

Other expressions in English with *to have* and *to take* can use either *tener* or *tomar*:

Necesito tomar(me)/tener un descanso.	I need to have/take a rest.
Quiero tomar(me)/tener unas vacaciones.	I want to take a vacation.

Tomar can use reflexive pronouns, but *tener* cannot.

The verb *coger* (*to take*) is used with the noun *vacaciones*. Reflexive pronouns are optional:

Ella quiere coger(se) unas vacaciones.	She wants to take a vacation.

Tener and *tomar* are not usually used with the gerund in these cases. The verb *descansar* (*to have a rest*) and the expression *estar de vacaciones* are preferable:

Ella está descansando.	She is resting/having/taking a rest.
Ellos están de vacaciones.	They are taking a vacation./They are on vacation.

In most other contexts, *to have* may be translated by *tener*, with the exception, of course, of when *to have* is the auxiliary verb *haber*:

Ellos no van a tener una reunión.	They aren't going to have a meeting.
Ella no puede tener novio.	She can't have a boyfriend.
No tenemos mucho tiempo.	We don't have much time.

Estoy teniendo algunos problemas.	I'm having some problems.
He leído este libro.	I have read this book.

To Be

In talking about measures of any kind, such as size, weight, or age, English uses the verb *to be*, but Spanish generally uses **tener**:

¿Cuántos años tienes?	How old are you?
¿Qué edad tienes?	
Tengo 20 años.	I am 20 years old.
¿Qué talla tienes?	What size are you?
Tengo la talla 50.	I'm a size 50.
¿Qué profundidad tiene?	How deep is it?
Tiene 100 pies de profundidad.	It is 100 feet deep.
¿Qué longitud tiene ese puente?	How long is that bridge?
Tiene 300 metros de longitud.	It is 300 meters long.
¿Qué anchura tiene esta habitación?	How wide is this room?
¿Qué peso tienes?/¿Cuál es tu peso?	What is your weight?

When talking about weight, the verb **pesar** is much more common:

¿Cuánto pesas?	How much do you weigh?
Peso 80 kilos.	I weigh 80 kilos.

When the preceding questions are asked with the pronoun **cuál**, the verb **ser** must be used:

¿Cuál es tu edad?	What is your age?
¿Cuál es tu estatura?	What is your height?/How tall are you?
¿Cuál es la longitud de ese barco?	What is the length of that ship?
¿Cuál es la anchura de esta habitación?	What is the width of this room?
¿Cuál es la profundidad de este lago?	What is the depth of this lake?
¿Cuál es tu talla?	What is your size?

The answers to these questions can use both **tener** and **ser**:

La longitud de este barco es de 100 metros.	The length of this ship is 100 meters.
Este barco tiene 100 metros de largo.	This ship is 100 meters long.
Mi estatura es un metro ochenta.	My height is one meter and 80 centimeters.
Tengo un metro ochenta de estatura.	I'm one meter eighty (centimeters) tall.

In measuring length, width, and height, the irregular verb **medir** (*to measure*) is commonly used:

Mido dos metros.	I am two meters tall.
Esta mesa mide un metró de ancho.	This table is one meter wide.

Other examples in which Spanish uses **tener**:

Tengo hambre.	I am hungry.
Ella tiene sed.	She is thirsty.
Tenemos miedo.	We are afraid.
Yo tengo razón.	I am right.

The general difference is that English usually uses adjectives, while Spanish uses nouns, although in translating *being hungry* and *being thirsty* it is possible (though less common) to use **estar** and adjectives:

Estoy hambriento.	I am hungry.
Ella está sedienta.	She is thirsty.

When talking about the weather, Spanish uses the verb **hacer** (in its third-person forms) and nouns. In this sense, **hacer** always acts as an impersonal verb (the subject is the impersonal *it*):

Hace calor.	It is hot.
Hace frío.	It is cold.
Hace sol.	It is sunny.
Hace viento.	It is windy.
Hace niebla.	It is foggy.

You can also say *Hay niebla,* which is more common.

Because **nublado** (*cloudy*) is an adjective, it must be used with the verb **estar**:

Está nublado.	It is cloudy.

The question *What's the weather like?* can be translated as **¿Cómo es el tiempo?** when it refers to the general aspects of the weather in a certain place, **¿Cómo está el tiempo?** when it refers to a specific day, and **¿Qué tiempo hace?** in both situations.

In translating the English construction *there is, there are, there was, there were,* etc., Spanish uses an impersonal variation of the verb **haber**. Note that the same form may be used for either singular or plural:

Hay mucho dinero.	There is a lot of money.
No hay tiempo.	There isn't any time.
¿Hay vino?	Is there any wine?
Hay muchos libros en la biblioteca.	There are many books in the library.
¿Hay muchos obreros en esa fábrica?	Are there many workers in that factory?

Auxiliaries are placed before the infinitive **haber**:

No puede haber tantos libros.	There can't be so many books.
Va a haber una reunión.	There is going to be a meeting.

The main function of the verb **haber** is to form perfect tenses, such as *I have eaten* and *she has passed.* This will be covered in Chapter 11. In many other cases, English and Spanish both use the verb *to be* (**ser** or **estar**):

Ella es mayor que tú.	She is older than you.
Estoy aterrado.	I am terrified.
Esa caja es muy pesada.	That box is very heavy.
Estoy preocupado.	I am worried.
¿Cuánto es?	How much is it?

Exercise 1

Fill in the blanks with appropriate verbs in the present, gerund, or infinitive.

1. Ese hombre _____ muchos más años que mi padre.

2. Ella _____ bastante mayor que tú.

3. Ese barco _____ una longitud muy superior a la de éste.

4. Mis padres están _____ un paseo.

5. El pobre chico _____ hambriento.

6. ¿Quiere usted _____ el desayuno en la terraza?

7. No debes _____ miedo. Yo estoy contigo.

8. Llevo tres meses a dieta. Ahora sólo _____ 70 kilos.

Exercise 2

Correct any mistakes.

1. Necesito estar unas vacaciones. Estoy muy cansado.

_____

2. ¿Por qué no les llevas a tomar un paseo?

_____

3. Esta noche vamos a cenar pollo con verdura.

_____

4. ¿Va usted a tener postre?

_____

5. Ese chaval es una estatura asombrosa.

_____

6. Necesito saber cuánto mide esta habitación.

_____

7. Yo ahora no tengo sed, así que no voy a dar nada.

_____

8. Hace mucho sol en el sur de España.

_____

Simple Past and Past Continuous (Indicative Mood)

As you know, there are two simple past tenses in the indicative mood, the imperfect (***el pretérito imperfecto***) and the preterit (***el pretérito indefinido***). These tenses usually cause great difficulty to students of Spanish, mainly because English only has one simple past tense. This chapter offers a thorough explanation of their specific uses in order to clarify the differences between the two.

El imperfecto

The ***imperfecto*** refers to a past action that wasn't completed or hadn't been finished. Therefore, the ***imperfecto*** is used to talk about habits and facts belonging to the past:

Yo no bebía mucho cuando era joven.	I didn't drink/used to drink very much when I was young.
La gente era más simpática.	People were/used to be more friendly.
Ellos vivían cerca de nosotros.	They lived/used to live near us.

The ***imperfecto*** of the irregular verb ***soler*** can be used to talk about habitual situations/actions:

Yo solía salir los viernes.	I used to go out on Fridays.
Ella no solía venir los martes.	She didn't use to come on Tuesdays.

But be careful, because **soler** can imply interruptions or pauses. A sentence like **Yo solía salir los viernes** can mean that *once in a while* the subject didn't go out on Fridays. This is why **soler** is not used to refer to habitual actions that happened all the time. Verbs like **vivir** (*to live*) and **ser** (when talking about professions/occupations, etc.), are not usually used with **soler**.

The **imperfecto** is also used to talk about actions that were still taking place at the moment referred to, and to express plans and intentions situated in the past (in English, this would be expressed with the past continuous):

Ella dormía cuando yo llegué.	She was sleeping when I arrived.
¿Qué hacías cuando te llamé?	What were you doing when I phoned you?
Yo tenía una cita con ella.	I had an appointment with her.

The verbs **ir** (*to go*) and **venir** (*to come*) are rarely used in the progressive form. *Was/were going to* translates as **iba a**, **ibas a**, etc., which is the **imperfecto** of the verb **ir** and the preposition **a**:

Ella iba a comprarlo.	She was going to buy it.
¿Ibas a hacerlo?	Were you going to do it?
Ellos iban a venir pero...	They were going to come but . . .
¿Dónde ibas?	Where were you going?

Pretérito indefinido

The **pretérito indefinido,** or **pretérito,** is most often used to talk about actions that were completed at the moment referred to in the past:

Yo cogí el dinero.	I took the money.
Ella no vino anoche.	She didn't come last night.
¿Qué hiciste ayer?	What did you do yesterday?

Very often this tense is used to refer to completed actions that had been habitual for some time:

Yo tuve una novia japonesa.	I had a Japanese girlfriend.
Yo tenía una novia japonesa.	

Ella fue mi secretaria.	She was my secretary.
Ella era mi secretaria.	

The ***imperfecto*** is never used when saying how long an action or a situation lasted. Compare:

Ella fue mi secretaria de 1980 a 1985.	She was my secretary from 1980 to 1985.
Ella era mi secretaria cuando llegaste.	She was my secretary when you arrived.

Pasado continuo (Past Continuous)

Just as there are two simple past tenses, there are also two continuous past tenses. The continuous tense formed with the ***imperfecto*** of the verb ***estar*** is mainly used to talk about actions that were still taking place at or around the past moment referred to. With very few exceptions, it is exactly the same as the English past continuous:

Ella estaba cantando.	She was singing.
¿Qué estabas haciendo?	What were you doing?

An important exception is that the continuous tense can't be used to talk about what someone was going to do (i.e., the "future of the past"), such as arrangements, plans, and intentions. The ***imperfecto*** is used instead:

Al día siguiente yo trabajaba de nueve a cinco.	I was working/I was going to work from nine to five the next day.

As you can see, there are two different tenses used to talk about past actions that were still taking place at the moment referred to, the ***imperfecto*** and the tense formed with the ***imperfecto*** of ***estar*** and a gerund. When the context is very clear, either can be used, although the continuous form is preferable, because the simple form often sounds literary and it might lead to confusion. ***Ella cantaba*** can mean that she was singing at that moment, or that she had the habit of singing. Without a clear context, this can be very confusing. ***Ella estaba cantando*** can only mean that she was singing at that moment.

The continuous form made with the ***pretérito indefinido*** of the verb ***estar*** doesn't coincide with the English past continuous. This tense can only refer to completed actions and is therefore almost equivalent to the ***pretérito simple*** (simple past). ***Yo estaba hablando con Pedro*** implies that I was still talking to Pedro at that moment. ***Yo estuve hablando con Pedro*** means that I had already finished talking to Pedro. In the first sentence, the emphasis is on the action still taking place at the moment referred to. In the second sentence, the form ***estuve*** refers to a finished action that had been in progress for some time. ***Yo hablé con Pedro*** means exactly the same as ***Yo estuve hablando con Pedro***. Choosing this continuous tense only depends on the speaker's wish to emphasize the fact that the action had been taking place for some time. This version of the past continuous sometimes translates as a past perfect continuous in English, mainly when its action is prior to another past action:

Antes de salir, Jorge estuvo estudiando durante tres horas.	Before going out, Jorge had been studying for three hours.

Confusing Cases

There are many cases in which the use of one tense or the other plays an important role in expressing whether the subject knew something in advance or not. In other cases, both tenses can be used, but there is usually an appreciable difference that depends on whether the speaker considers the action completed or still taking place. The examples and explanations that follow will clarify this:

Ella tenía una reunión.	She was having a meeting.
Ella tuvo una reunión.	She had a meeting.

In the first sentence, either the meeting hadn't started yet or it was taking place at that moment. The second sentence simply states that the meeting had already taken place.

Ella tenía que hacerlo.	She had to do it.
Ella tuvo que hacerlo.	She had to do it.

In the first sentence, the obligation to do something was known in advance. It doesn't say whether the action was completed or not (the context usually makes this clear). In the second sentence, the action was completed because, at that very moment, the subject felt that she had an obligation to do it.

Yo tenía problemas.	I had/was having problems.
Yo tuve problemas.	I had problems.

The first sentence says that my problems hadn't been solved yet at the moment referred to (I still had them at that moment). The second sentence refers to my problems as if they no longer existed at that moment (they had already been solved). Sometimes the difference between one tense and another is completely subjective.

No fui porque no tenía que ir.	I didn't go because I didn't have to go.
No tuve que hacerlo, porque ella vino.	I didn't have to do it, because she came.

In the first sentence, I didn't go because I knew in advance that I didn't have to go. In the second sentence, something happened which caused me not to have to do it.

Remember: ***No tenía que*** expresses lack of obligation to do something known in advance. ***No tuve que*** expresses lack of obligation to do something, because at that very moment something happened or was happening.

Ella iba a la playa todos los días.	She went/used to go to the beach every day.
Ella iba a la playa cuando él la vio.	She was going to the beach when he saw her.
Ella fue a la playa.	She went to the beach.

The first sentence is a habit and therefore the ***imperfecto*** must be used. In the second sentence, she was on her way to the beach when something else happened. The third sentence states that she had reached the beach on a specific day.

Ellos estaban en mi casa.	They were in my house.
Ellos estuvieron en mi casa.	They were in my house.

In the first sentence, they were still in my house at the moment referred to. In the second sentence, they had already left. The choice of tense depends on the speaker's intention. Either I want to refer to something while they were still in my house or I just want to say that they were in my house but left.

Ella quería comprarlo.	She wanted to buy it.
Ella quiso comprarlo.	She wanted to buy it.

In the first sentence, she had had the wish to buy it for some time. How long she had had the wish is not important; what matters is that she already knew that she wanted to buy it. The second sentence only refers to that very moment. It doesn't imply anything known in advance. Whether she bought it or not will depend on the context.

The ***imperfecto*** of the verb ***hay*** (*there is/there are*) is ***había*** (*there was/there were*). The ***pretérito indefinido*** is ***hubo*** (very often translated as *there had been*):

Había un hombre en la cocina.	There was a man in the kitchen.
Hubo un accidente.	There had been an accident.

Había considers the action as still happening. ***Hubo*** refers to something that had already taken place:

Aquella mañana había una reunión.	There was a meeting that morning.
Aquella mañana hubo una reunión.	There had been a meeting that morning.

In the first example, the meeting hadn't started yet or was taking place at that moment. In the second example, the meeting had already finished.

In many cases, both forms can be used without a difference of meaning:

¿Había mucha gente en la boda?	Were there many people at the wedding?
¿Hubo mucha gente en la boda?	

In such a case, the difference is subjective. In the first sentence, the speaker can see the wedding taking place. In the second sentence, the speaker considers the wedding as something in the past.

When narrating, or saying what was happening at that moment, the form **había** is usual, although **hubo** is possible if the narrator refers to a previous moment:

Abrí la puerta. No había nadie dentro, pero había un olor...	I opened the door. There was nobody inside, but there was a smell . . .
Yo sabía que hubo un asesinato en esa habitación.	I knew that there had been a murder in that room.

Exercise 1
Underline the appropriate tense.

1. El otro día *tuve/tenía* una experiencia muy extraña.

2. Carlos *supo/sabía* que él *tenía/tuvo* que hacer un examen ese día, pero *decidía/decidió* quedarse en casa simulando estar enfermo.

3. Mientras Ana *preparaba/preparó* la cena, su marido *bañó/bañaba* a los niños.

4. Paco me *contaba/contó* que él *quería/quiso* comprar una casa en México, pero no *tenía/tuvo* suficiente dinero todavía.

5. Al día siguiente las tiendas *fueron/iban* a abrir un poco más tarde.

6. Cuando Antonio *terminaba/terminó* de desayunar, *cogió/cogía* los libros y se *marchó/marchaba*.

7. Camino del colegio *tropezaba/tropecé* con los hermanos de Luisa. Me *decían/dijeron* que *esperaban/esperaron* el autobús para ir al parque de atracciones.

8. El pequeño *dejó/dejaba* caer una maceta justo en el momento en que un hombre *pasó/pasaba* por debajo del balcón.

9. Unos hombres *bebían/bebieron* en el bar tranquilamente. De repente *entró/entraba* un forastero que les *preguntó/preguntaba* si los coches que *había/hubo* en la puerta *eran/fueron* suyos.

10. El profesor nos *explicaba/explicó* que ese material no *conducía/condujo* la electricidad.

Exercise 2

Fill in the blanks with the *imperfecto*, *pretérito indefinido*, or continuous form of the *imperfecto* or the *pretérito* of the verbs in parentheses.

Cuando _____ (yo venir) hacia la oficina, un policía de tráfico me _____ (parar). Se _____ (bajar) de la moto y se _____ (acercar) a mi coche. Cuando _____ (él estar) a la altura de mi ventanilla, yo le _____ (preguntar) que qué _____ (pasar). Él me _____ (responder) que yo no _____ (llevar) puesto el cinturón de seguridad. De repente yo me _____ (poner) muy nervioso, ya que yo sí lo _____ (llevar) puesto, así que le _____ (yo hacer) saber que _____ (él deber) estar un error. El policía me _____ (mirar) con cara de asombro y _____ (empezar) a darme gritos. La situación _____ (ser) realmente extraña. Incluso _____ (yo llegar) a pensar que se _____

(tratar) de una broma. Me _____ (bajar) del coche e _____

(intentar) calmarle. Mientras yo _____ (hacer) esto, otros dos

policías _____ (aparecer) con sus motos. Le _____ (ellos

coger) fuertemente y le _____ (poner) las esposas. Al parecer, el

individuo _____ (ser) un loco que se _____ (hacer) pasar por

policía de tráfico con una moto robada.

Confusing Verbs, Part 3

Discutir

The verb ***discutir*** means *to discuss* and *to argue*:

Tenemos que discutir el precio primero.	We have to discuss the price first.
Ellos siempre están discutiendo.	They are always arguing.

When the reason why the subjects of the sentence argue is mentioned, the preposition ***por*** is used:

Ellos discutieron por los niños.	They argued because of the children.

Conversar

Conversar actually means *to have a conversation*. In some Latin American countries (Mexico, for example), speakers often use the verb ***platicar***, which is never used in Spain.

Preguntar

The verb ***preguntar*** can't be used to translate *to ask a question*. ***Hacer una pregunta*** is used instead:

Ella preguntó si podía encender la tele.	She asked if she could turn on the TV.

¿Puedo hacerte una pregunta?   Can I ask you a question?

To ask for somebody translates as **preguntar por**:

Pregunté por Carlos.   I asked for Carlos.

Preguntar por is also used to ask for the way to a place:

Ellos preguntaron por el camino a   They asked for the way to the
la oficina de correos.   post office.

The reflexive verb **preguntarse** means *to wonder* in English:

Me pregunto qué vas a hacer ahora.   I wonder what you are going to
do now.

Aterrar

The verb **aterrar** can be used as a transitive verb:

Ella dice que yo les aterro.   She says that I terrify them.

But this verb is most often used like **gustar** and **encantar**:

A mí me aterra la idea de trabajar   I'm terrified by the idea of
allí.   working there.

Pelear

Pelear means *to fight* (physical) and *to argue* (oral). It is most often used
with reflexive pronouns:

Ellos se pelearon por el dinero.   They fought/argued about the
money.

The context will make it clear whether it was a physical fight or just an
argument.

Arriesgar

Arriesgar can be used both with and without reflexive pronouns. If it is used with reflexive pronouns, this verb is always followed by the preposition **a**:

Ella no quiere arriesgar su fortuna.	She doesn't want to risk her fortune.
Ella no quiere arriesgarse a perder el dinero que su padre le dio.	She doesn't want to risk losing the money that her father gave her.

Continuar

Continuar (*to continue*) is one of the many regular verbs with a stress change in their conjugation (**yo continúo, tú continúas, él continúa,** etc.). If another verb follows, the second verb is always a gerund:

Puedes continuar trabajando.	You can continue working.

Prestar

The verb **prestar** is often replaced by the verb **dejar**:

¿Puedes prestarme 20 dólares?	Can you lend me 20 dollars?
¿Puedes dejarme 20 dólares?	

The verb **prestar** is preferable to the verb **coger/tomar prestado** (*to borrow*):

¿Me puedes prestar el diccionario?	Can you lend me the dictionary?/Can I borrow the dictionary from you?

You can say **¿Puedo coger prestado <u>el/tu</u> periódico?**, but it is incorrect to say **¿Puedo coger prestado el periódico <u>de ti</u>?**

Montar

The verb **montar** (*to ride*) requires the preposition **en** when the type of vehicle follows, but with **caballo** the preposition **a** must be used:

Ella monta muy bien en bicicleta.	She is very good at riding bikes.
Ella monta en bicicleta muy bien.	(*Literally:* She rides bikes very well.)
A mí me encanta montar en tren.	I love riding on trains.
Ella estaba montando a caballo.	She was riding on horseback.

Mostrar

In some contexts, **mostrar** means the same as **enseñar**. **Mostrar** is a stem-changing verb (**o** to **ue**):

¿Puede usted enseñarme/mostrarme la nueva colección?	Can you show me the new collection?
¿Le muestro la nueva colección?	Shall I show you the new collection?

Enseñar can mean *to teach*, but **mostrar** cannot:

Yo enseño español en la universidad.   I teach Spanish at college.

Saber/Conocer

Both **saber** and **conocer** translate as *to know*. The basic difference between them is that **saber** is the result of a learning process. **Saber** is more often used to refer to data (address, phone number, name, etc.) and is therefore related to memorizing details. **Conocer** is the result of both a prior experience and a learning process and is therefore related to having seen it, having read it, having heard it, having learned it, or having been there before. All this means that in many cases both verbs can be used without significant differences of meaning:

Yo no sé/conozco el nombre de esa chica.	I don't know that girl's name.
Ella conoce París muy bien.	She knows Paris very well.
(*Ella sabe París...* is incorrect.)	

Él sabe/conoce mi dirección.	He knows my address.
Él conoce mi casa.	He knows my house.

Conocer can't be used with **que** (*that*) or **si** (*if*). **Saber** is used instead:

¿Sabes que Juan tiene una hija?	Do you know that Juan has a daughter?

Note: Use **conocer** when talking about places, situations, experiences, and people, and to indicate that something seems familiar.

The verb **saber** is usually used with reflexive pronouns when talking about lessons and school activities:

Yo me sé la lección muy bien.	I know the lesson very well (*because I have studied it*).

When talking about the ability to do something, English uses the verb *can*. Spanish uses the verb **saber** (never **conocer**), especially when the ability is the result of a learning process:

Ella no sabe nadar.	She can't swim.
Yo sé tocar la guitarra.	I can play the guitar.
¿Sabes conducir?	Can you drive?

It is possible to use the verb **poder**, but then the meaning changes. **Saber nadar** implies that the person referred to *knows how to swim*. **Poder nadar** only indicates the possibility of swimming at that moment. **Ella no puede nadar** can mean that *she is not allowed to swim*, or that *something prevents her from swimming*, but it says nothing about knowing how to swim.

Pedir

Pedir (*to ask for something*) doesn't need to be followed by a preposition:

Él me pidió dinero.	He asked me for some money.
Nosotros no pedimos nada.	We didn't ask for anything.
Ella pidió ver al director.	She asked to see the manager.

Negar/Negarse

Negar means *to deny*. **Negarse a** is reflexive and uses the preposition **a**; it means *to refuse*:

Él negó pertenecer a la banda.	He denied belonging to the gang.
Ella se negó a venir.	She refused to come.

Seguir

Seguir has two meanings in English. It translates as *to follow* and as *to go on* (*to continue, to keep on*, etc.). When it means *to go on*, it is followed by nouns, pronouns, or gerunds, but never infinitives:

Alguien nos está siguiendo.	Somebody is following us.
Debes seguir con los ejercicios.	You must go on with the exercises.
No puedes seguir haciendo eso.	You can't go on doing that.

Exercise 1

Underline the correct option.

1. ¿Por qué no *conversamos/discutimos* esto en privado?

2. Me *aterran/arriesgan* las arañas.

3. En ese colegio me *enseñaron/mostraron* a hablar en inglés.

4. Ella me *preguntó/pidió* si yo vivía con mis padres.

5. Yo le *pregunté/pedí* un pequeño favor.

6. No puedes *negarte/negar* a participar en esa carrera.

7. Nosotros no *sabemos/conocemos* ese lugar.

8. Antonio *sabe/conoce* tocar el violín muy bien.

9. Ella no quiso *arriesgar/arriesgarse* a ser suspendida.

10. Ellos *negaron/se negaron* ser cómplices de los ladrones.

Exercise 2

Four of the following sentences contain one or more errors. Correct them.

1. Creo que todavía no te sabes la teoría muy bien. _____

2. El médico me dijo que (yo) no sabía montar en bicicleta, porque mi tobillo no estuvo curado todavía. _____

3. La mujer me preguntó la calle Tejedores. _____

4. Les pregunté la lección, pero no se la supieron. _____

5. Pedí las entradas por teléfono. _____

6. ¿Me puedes mostrar algunos modelos más? _____

7. Me niego a estar relacionado con el robo que se cometió. _____

8. Sé tocar varios instrumentos musicales. _____

9. No sé cómo llegar a ese lugar. _____

10. ¿Por qué no continuaste caminar? _____

The Verb *Haber* and Perfect Tenses

As you know, the compound, or perfect, tenses with the verb **haber** can only be followed by past participles. This way you can form tenses such as the **pretérito perfecto compuesto** (similar to the English present perfect), which is formed with the present tense of the verb **haber** and a past participle, and the **pretérito pluscuamperfecto** (similar to the English past perfect), which is formed with the **imperfecto** of the verb **haber** and a past participle:

He comido en ese restaurante.	I have eaten in that restaurant.
¿Has visto a Pablo?	Have you seen Pablo?
He estado entrenando.	I have been training.
Ella no había terminado.	She hadn't finished.
Ellos habían estado hablando.	They had been talking.

Despite the many similarities in tense formation and usage between English and Spanish, perfect tenses require special attention because there are also important differences between the two that cause confusion and lead to mistakes.

Pretérito perfecto

Although this tense and the English present perfect are formed in the same way, there are important differences in their uses. Both, however, refer to a past action that is related to the present:

He bebido demasiado.	I have drunk too much. (*today, at this party, etc.*)

Hemos comprado un coche.	We have bought a car. (*this week, this month, this year, etc.*)
No has estudiado mucho este trimestre.	You haven't studied hard this term.

In English, if an action that took place at ten o'clock in the morning is referred to at seven o'clock in the evening, the simple past, which is also known as the preterit, is used. Spanish requires the compound tense ***pretérito perfecto***, although in most of the Latin American countries the simple past (preterit) is used:

Esta mañana he visto a Juan.	I have seen Juan this morning. (*If it is said during the morning.*) I saw Juan this morning. (*If it is said in the afternoon or in the evening.*)

In Venezuela, for example, speakers prefer ***Esta mañana vi a Juan.***

In English, when something is noticed for the first time, the present perfect is used, but if the speaker goes on talking about the same fact, the preterit is used. In Spanish, the present perfect (***pretérito perfecto***) is used in both cases:

Alguien ha dejado la puerta abierta. Yo no he sido.	Somebody has left the door open. It wasn't me.

In fact, the ***pretérito perfecto*** is used to refer to past actions that have taken place in a period of time that can still be considered present or recent (this morning, today, this month, etc.). The reference to a present period of time doesn't have to be mentioned in the sentence. ***Hemos comprado la casa*** (*We have bought the house*) means that the house has been bought in a period of time that the speaker considers recent or related to the present. It could have been this month, this year, or within a period of time that goes from a certain moment in the past up to now (since a friend's last visit some months ago, for example).

In English, it isn't possible to use the present perfect in questions with *when*. In Spanish, the ***pretérito perfecto*** is used if the question is in any way related to the speaker's present. If the question is connected to a past context, then the ***pretérito indefinido*** is used. In many Latin American countries speakers prefer the ***pretérito indefinido*** in both situations:

¿Cuándo has llegado?	When did you arrive?
¿Cuándo llegaste?	When did you arrive?

The first question is asked of someone whose arrival was unknown to the speaker. The second question is asked when the speaker knows that the person spoken to arrived some time ago. This means that the ***pretérito perfecto*** is always used in questions when there is no prior information. The ***pretérito indefinido*** is used when it is known that the action took place in the past.

Similarly to English, the ***pretérito perfecto*** is not used with words that refer to the past (*yesterday, last month,* etc.). Instead, the ***pretérito indefinido*** is used:

Ayer estuve en la playa.	I was on the beach yesterday.
Lo compré el mes pasado.	I bought it last month.

This means that the ***pretérito perfecto*** is used to refer to past actions related to the speaker's present, or actions considered to be recent, but without mentioning exactly when they occurred. If the past moment is mentioned, the ***pretérito indefinido*** must be used:

Hemos comprado la casa. La compramos después de tu última visita hace seis meses.	We have bought the house. We bought it after your last visit six months ago.

The question now is: Where is the limit? What do Spanish speakers consider recent or related to their present? There is no exact answer to this question because the difference between recent and not recent is subjective on most occasions. It usually depends on the speaker's perspective, but, on the whole, significant *time frontiers* (a year, for example) can be a help. Spanish speakers probably wouldn't use the ***pretérito perfecto*** when referring to something done a year ago or longer.

As in English, the *pretérito perfecto* is also used in sentences that embrace an entire lifetime:

¿Has comido pulpo alguna vez?	Have you ever eaten octopus?
Nunca he visto esa película.	I have never seen that film.

Here is a summary of the different uses of the *pretérito perfecto*:

- Use the *pretérito perfecto* with words that show duration of time and actions that sound as though they are in the present:

<u>Este año</u> no hemos ahorrado mucho *dinero.*	We haven't saved much money this year.
<u>Hoy</u> no he visto a Pedro.	I haven't seen Pedro today.

- Use the *pretérito perfecto* in questions related to recent periods of time if it is unknown when the action took place or if it is unknown whether the action has taken place or not. This includes questions with **cuándo**:

¿Has terminado tus deberes?	Have you finished your homework?
¿Cuándo has terminado tus deberes?	When did you finish your homework?

- Use the *pretérito perfecto* to talk about actions that seem recent or relatively recent (a year ago or less):

He aprobado todos mis exámenes.	I have passed all my exams. (*having* **este año** *in mind*)

- Use the *pretérito perfecto* to talk about actions and to enumerate events and actions that have taken place within a period that embraces an entire lifetime or an important part of it:

Hemos criado a cinco hijos.	We have brought up five children. (*since our wedding*)
Hemos sido muy felices juntos.	We have been very happy together. (*up to now*)

Be careful with sentences in which the speaker knows when something happened but requires further details:

¿A qué hora ha llegado el avión?	What time did the plane arrive?
¿A qué hora llegó el avión?	What time did the plane arrive?

In the first question, the speaker knows that the plane has arrived today (present). In the second question, the speaker knows that the plane arrived yesterday or before yesterday. The only detail the speaker doesn't know is the time of arrival.

There are many native speakers who prefer the ***pretérito indefinido*** in all the situations previously described, but don't let this be an excuse to avoid learning the ***pretérito perfecto***. This tense is in common use (especially in Spain), and it is needed to express nuances that the ***pretérito indefinido*** is not able to offer.

Pretérito perfecto compuesto continuo

This tense is in many aspects very similar to the English **present perfect continuous**:

He estado entrenando.	I have been training.
Ella ha estado pintando la casa.	She has been painting the house.
Ha estado lloviendo.	It has been raining.

It is used to talk about actions that have been in progress for some time up to now. The focus is on the action itself, not on the action being finished or not. Compare:

He estado traduciendo toda la mañana.	I have been translating all morning.
He traducido dos cartas esta mañana.	I have translated two letters this morning.

The first sentence only refers to the action of translating. In the second sentence, the attention is focused on the letters translated.

Many who are learning Spanish find it difficult to understand the exact difference between this tense and the ***pretérito perfecto continuo*** (***yo*** *estuve trabajando, tú estuviste hablando,* etc.). The ***pretérito per-fecto continuo*** doesn't exist in English. A sentence like *I was sleeping* means that I was still doing it at the moment referred to and corresponds to **Yo estaba durmiendo**, not to **Yo estuve durmiendo**, which implies that I finished doing it. To avoid unnecessary mistakes, apply the same rules that explain the difference between the ***pretérito perfecto*** (*he hablado*) and the ***pretérito indefinido*** (*hablé*):

He estado leyendo en español esta semana.	I have been reading in Spanish this week.
Ayer estuve hablando con ellos.	I talked to them yesterday.
He estado trabajando mucho últimamente.	I have been working very hard lately.
Ayer estuve trabajando de 8 a 12.	I worked from 8 to 12 yesterday.

Latin Americans prefer the past simple of **estar** and gerund forms to the ***pretérito perfecto compuesto continuo***.

Pretérito pluscuamperfecto

The ***pretérito pluscuamperfecto*** (including the continuous form) is very similar to the English past perfect:

Ella me dijo que su hijo no había terminado sus deberes.	She told me that her son hadn't finished his homework.
La chica nos dijo que su padre no había estado trabajando esa mañana.	The girl told us that her father hadn't been working that morning.
Yo ya había terminado mis ejercicios cuando ellos llegaron.	I had already finished my exercises when they arrived.

In reported speech (i.e., what the speaker says another speaker said), the ***pluscuamperfecto*** is often replaced by the ***pretérito indefinido simple*** or the ***pretérito perfecto continuo***:

Ella me dijo que su hijo no terminó sus deberes.	She told me that her son hadn't finished (didn't finish) his homework.

La chica nos dijo que su padre no estuvo trabajando esa mañana.	The girl told us that her father hadn't been working that morning.

The tense formed with the **pretérito indefinido** of the verb **haber** (**yo hube**, **tú hubiste**, etc.) is called the **pretérito anterior**. This tense is used to refer to actions that were completed before another action started (almost simultaneously and usually accompanied by **cuando** and similar words), and it is confined to very formal speech and literature. It is usually replaced by the **pretérito indefinido**:

arranqué	I started
Cuando <u>hube arrancado</u> el tractor me marché al pueblo. (highly unusual)	When <u>I had started</u> the tractor I left for the town.

It must not be confused with the **pluscuamperfecto**, which is not usually accompanied by the word **cuando**:

Cuando llegué a la habitación, alguien había puesto flores en la mesa.	When I arrived at the room, somebody had put flowers on the table.

Confusing Cases

Although there are important similarities between English and Spanish with regard to the use of perfect tenses, there are some cases that need special attention. A good example is the English construction *have just* + past participle, which translates as **acabar de** + infinitive:

Acabo de comer.	I have just eaten.
Ella acaba de terminar.	She has just finished.
Él acababa de llegar.	He had just arrived.
Ellos acababan de comprarlo.	They had just bought it.

Another important case is when the speaker wants to express something that started in the past and is still being done in the present. A sentence like *I have lived there for 20 years* implies that the subject still lives there. Translated literally, this sentence would be ***He vivido allí durante 20 años***, which can mean that the subject no longer lives there. Remember that the ***pretérito perfecto*** can be used to talk about actions that embrace a period up to the moment of speaking, and to talk about actions that have been completed in the recent past. To express in Spanish that an action started in the past and continues at the moment of speaking, it is much better to use the ***presente*** or the ***imperfecto*** for past contexts than the ***pretérito perfecto*** or the ***pluscuamperfecto***:

Vivo allí desde hace 20 años.	I have lived there for 20 years.
Lo tengo desde ayer.	I've had it since yesterday.
Ella vivía allí desde hacía mucho tiempo.	She had lived there for a long time.
Estaban casados desde hacía diez años.	They had been married for ten years.

Perfect tenses can be confusing or lead to mistakes in this type of sentence. Besides, there are many cases in which it is not possible to use perfect tenses to refer to actions that started in the past and are still taking place at the moment of speaking.

The verb ***llevar*** and gerund forms can be used to translate *have/had been + -ing* to refer to actions that started in the past and are still taking place:

Llevo trabajando aquí dos días.	I have been working here for two days.
Ella llevaba intentándolo dos horas.	She had been trying for two hours.

It is more common to place the reference to time between ***llevar*** and the gerund:

Llevo dos días haciendo esto.	I have been doing this for two days.
Juan llevaba un año estudiando.	John had been studying for a year.

To express *for* with duration of time (*for a week*, *for a month*, etc.), use ***desde hace*** for the present and ***desde hacía*** for the past. To express *since*, use ***desde que***: ***desde que la vi*** (*since I saw her*), which must be followed or preceded by a clause. Note that these expressions with ***desde*** are not commonly used with the verb ***llevar***:

Tengo esto desde que tenía tu edad.	I've had this since I was your age.
Desde que la vi me enamoré de ella.	Ever since I saw her I fell in love with her.
Lo sé desde hace dos días.	I have known for two days.
Ella estaba allí desde hacía un año.	She had been there for a year.

Note: The English construction *it's (been)* + period of time + *since* + preterit or present perfect is equivalent to ***hace*** + period of time + ***que*** + negative simple present:

Hace siglos que no les veo.	It's (been) ages since I saw them.
Hace siglos que no como aquí.	It's (been) ages since I ate here.
Hace seis años que no hablo con mi hermano.	It's been six years since I've talked to my brother.

Questions can begin with ***cuánto tiempo hace que***, ***cuánto hace que***, and ***desde cuándo*** without changing the meaning:

¿Cuánto hace que lo sabes?	How long have you known?
¿Desde cuándo estás enfermo?	How long have you been ill?

Negative sentences like ***No fumo desde hace dos días*** (*I haven't smoked for two days*) are equivalent to structures with the verb ***llevar*** and the preposition ***sin*** followed by the infinitive:

No visito a mi madre desde hace un año.	I haven't visited my mother for a year.
Llevo un año sin visitar a mi madre.	

When the sentence only refers to actions completed in the past, *for* is translated by ***durante***:

Estuve allí durante dos días.	I was there for two days.
Les busqué durante dos semanas.	I looked for them for two weeks.

The infinitive of the verb **hay** (*there is/there are*) is **haber**. This verb is like two verbs in one: one is an auxiliary verb (*to have*) and is used to conjugate perfect tenses, and the other is used to express *there is, there were, there will be, there have been,* etc. When it is used with these meanings in Spanish, other verb forms are placed before the infinitive **haber**:

No puede haber nadie.	There can't be anybody (there).
Va a haber una pelea.	There is going to be a fight.

Perfect tenses of the verb **haber** (*ha habido, había habido,* etc.) are formed by placing the different tenses of the auxiliary verb **haber** before the past participle **habido**:

Ha habido un accidente.	There has been an accident.
Había habido problemas.	There had been some problems.

In these examples, auxiliaries can never be plural; **_Han habido_** is incorrect.

Exercise 1
Make any corrections.

1. Juan trabaja en esa fábrica. Ha trabajado allí desde 1990.

_____

2. Nunca he estado en el norte del país.

_____

3. Estuve hablando con Ana cuando me viste.

_____

4. La semana pasada no hemos ganado nada.

_____

5. Ella ya había terminado de cenar cuando llegaron sus amigos.

_____

6. Llevo dos años intentando conseguir otro empleo.

_____

7. Juan nos ha conocido desde hace un par de años.

_____

8. Aún no hemos conseguido hablar con el director.

_____

Exercise 2

Fill in the blanks with an appropriate form of the verbs in parentheses.

1. ¡Hombre, Arturo! ¡Estás aquí! ¿Cuánto tiempo hace que nos

   _____ (esperar)?

2. Hace dos días _____ (comprar) un televisor de plasma.

3. Yo _____ (estudiar) antes de salir.

4. _____ (haber) varios temblores de tierra esta semana.

5. Ella dice que no _____ (tener) tiempo suficiente para

   terminar el ejercicio que tú le _____ (mandar) ayer.

6. Cuando me _____ (levantar) no _____ (haber) nadie,

   pero pude ver que alguien _____ (revolver) mis cosas.

7. ¿Cuánto tiempo _____ (llevar) tú casado cuando tu mujer te

   _____ (dejar)?

Exercise 3

Underline the correct option.

1. Hoy no *he comido/comí* con mis padres.

2. Ayer *tuve/he tenido* que ir al dentista.

3. *Visité/He visitado* cinco países hasta ahora.

4. *Tengo/He tenido* este coche desde hace dos años.

5. ¿Cuánto tiempo hace que *has salido/sales* con esa chica?

6. El profesor ya *terminó/había terminado* de explicar la lección cuando yo llegué.

7. Para esa hora, la película ya *había empezado/empezó*.

8. ¿Por qué estás tan rojo? ¿*Estuviste/Has estado* corriendo?

9. No me gustan los resultados que *obtuviste/has obtenido* este trimestre.

10. *Hubo/había* un robo en una joyería la semana pasada.

Exercise 4

Rewrite the following sentences without changing the meaning.

1. Llevo dos días sin hablar con ella.

No _____

2. Llevo un año sin montar en moto.

Hace _____

3. No bebo alcohol desde hace un año.

Llevo _____

4. No vengo al pueblo desde hace varios meses.

Llevo _____

5. Hace más de un mes que no sé nada de él.

No _____

Future and Conditional

Spanish speakers usually follow the same thought patterns as English speakers do when talking about the future. Both use different tenses to refer to future actions or facts. Important aspects such as plans, intentions, predictions, etc. will determine which tense to use.

Talking About the Future

The Spanish future tense is not usually used to talk about intentions, plans, or arrangements. Instead, the present or the construction *ir a* (in the present) + infinitive is used:

Mañana voy a Granada.	I'm going to Granada tomorrow.
La semana que viene no trabajo.	I'm not working next week.
Voy a comprar una casa.	I'm going to buy a house.

Remember that the Spanish present tense requires words that indicate a context that refers to the future. Otherwise, the present tense can only refer to the present. ***Juego al tenis*** can only mean *I play tennis* (a habit), but ***Mañana juego al tenis*** (*I'm playing tennis tomorrow*) is a future plan.

The future tense is used in general predictions and to indicate future possibility:

Habrá chubascos en el norte.	There will be showers in the north.
Tendremos que vender el coche.	We will have to sell the car.

In predictions, the present of the construction *ir a* + infinitive is usually used when there is a high degree of certainty:

Va a llover.	It is going to rain.
Ellos van a ganar las elecciones.	They are going to win the elections.

In predictions with a high degree of certainty, the future tense can also be used, especially when the speaker wants to express that the future action will take place because it always, or nearly always, does:

Ganarán los socialistas, como de costumbre.	The Socialists will win, as usual.

In such sentences, the speaker very often expresses a lack of power to change the situation.

The present is often used in predictions when the speaker expresses absolute conviction:

Los socialistas ganan, estoy seguro.	The Socialists are going to win, I'm sure.
Mañana llueve aquí.	It's going to rain here tomorrow.

The future tense is used in promises, although the present (or the present of *ir a* + infinitive) can also be used:

Te prometo que no lo haré.	I promise you that I won't do it.
Te prometo que no lo hago.	
Te prometo que no lo voy a hacer.	
Te prometo que vendré.	I promise you that I will come.
Te prometo que vengo.	
Te prometo que voy a venir.	

Strong determination is often expressed by means of the future tense, though the present and the present of *ir a* + infinitive are also possible:

¡No iré a esa fiesta!	I won't go to that party!
¡No voy a esa fiesta!	
¡No voy a ir a esa fiesta!	

In English, when a decision is taken at the moment of speaking, the verb *will* is used. Spanish uses the present:

Alguien tiene que ir al	Somebody has to go to the
supermercado.	supermarket.
Yo voy.	I'll go.

The future tense is possible in this case, but the present is much more common.

As in English, the present is used to talk about future actions that belong to scheduled activities, timetables, etc.:

¿A qué hora abren las tiendas?	What time do the shops open?
¿A qué hora empieza la película?	What time does the film start?
¿Cuándo sale el avión?	When does the plane leave?

Concessions made to people are usually expressed by the future tense, but the present of *ir a* + infinitive is also possible:

¡De acuerdo! ¡Tendrás tu bicicleta!	All right! You will have your bike!
¡De acuerdo! ¡Vas a tener tu *bicicleta!*	All right! You're going to have your bike!

The future in Spanish is often used to guess what is already happening at the present moment and to suppose that an action is taking place at or around the moment of speaking:

¿Por qué no puede venir Jorge?	Why can't Jorge come?
No sé. Tendrá deberes.	I don't know. Maybe he has homework.

The Spanish **futuro continuo** and the English future continuous are equivalent when talking about actions that you think will be happening at a certain time in the future:

No debes visitarles a las ocho,	You shouldn't visit them at eight,
porque estarán cenando.	because they will be having dinner.

Para esta hora el martes que viene estaremos volando hacia París.	By this time next Tuesday we will be flying to Paris.
Estarán trabajando si les visitas a las once de la mañana.	They will be working if you visit them at eleven o'clock in the morning.

The *futuro continuo* can't be used to talk about decisions or plans. A sentence like *I will be driving into town at six, so I can give you a lift* can't be translated into Spanish by means of the *futuro continuo*, nor can this tense be used in questions like *Will you be using your car tonight?* In both cases the present of *ir a* + infinitive should be used: *Voy a llegar a la ciudad a las seis, así que te puedo llevar. ¿Vas a usar tu coche esta noche?*

The future tense of the auxiliary verb *haber* and a past participle form the Spanish future perfect (*futuro perfecto*):

Ellos habrán terminado para las seis.	They will have finished by six.

The future perfect is used to talk about actions that will have been completed by some time in the future:

Para el próximo agosto ya habré terminado el libro.	By next August I will already have finished the book.
Supongo que tu profesor habrá corregido tu examen para mañana.	I suppose that your teacher will have graded your exam by tomorrow.

The *futuro perfecto* is also used to suppose that an action has already taken place and to express what probably happened in the past:

No habrán muerto en vano.	They won't have died in vain.
Son las nueve de la noche. Supongo que ellos ya habrán cenado.	It is nine o'clock in the evening. I suppose that they have had dinner already.

The future perfect of **estar** combines with a gerund to form the ***futuro perfecto continuo*** (future perfect continuous), with similar uses to the cases previously cited:

Supongo que habréis estado conduciendo todo el día. Parecéis muy cansados.	I suppose that you have been driving all day. You look very tired.
Si haces eso, habrás estado trabajando para nada.	If you do that, you will have been working for nothing.

Important Differences

The English verb *will* is always translated by **querer** when making requests:

¿Quieres cerrar la puerta?	Will you close the door?
¿Quieres callarte?	Will you be quiet?

Will can also be translated by **querer** in contexts that convey the idea of refusal:

La he llamado por teléfono, pero no quiere escucharme.	I have phoned her, but she won't listen to me.

The Spanish future tense is not used in sentences like *The car won't start*. To say that objects "refuse" to work, use the present:

La lavadora no para de gotear.	The washing machine won't stop leaking.
Este bolígrafo no escribe.	This pen won't write.

Shall is not translated in sentences that refer to offers, proposals, or suggestions. Spanish uses the present in such cases:

¿Te ayudo?	Shall I help you?
¿Nos vamos al cine?	Shall we go to the cinema?

The Conditional (*Condicional*)

Spanish uses the **condicional** much like English uses the conditional tense. The following examples show the similarities between both languages:

Yo no haría eso.	I wouldn't do that.
Si eso fuera verdad, yo estaría trabajando ahora.	If that were true, I would be working now.
Yo no habría hecho eso.	I wouldn't have done that.
Si tus niños hubieran venido, habrían estado jugando con los míos.	If your children had come, they would have been playing with mine.

Since Spanish doesn't have modal verbs (e.g., *will, can, must*), a verb like **deber** (*must*) can be conjugated in any tense:

Debes estudiar.	You must study.
Deberías venir.	You should come.
Deberías haber cogido un taxi.	You should have taken a taxi.

In the preceding examples, *should* is, more or less, the conditional of *must*. Other contexts in which English uses *should* require different tenses in Spanish. A sentence like *She asked me if she should help me* is similar to the sentence *Shall I help you?*, but as reported speech. Because Spanish uses the present to translate questions with *shall I/we*, the **imperfecto** is required in reported speech. The verb **debería** is therefore *not* used in such cases:

Ella me preguntó si me prestaba su ordenador.	She asked me if she should lend me her computer.
Yo les pregunté si les traía algo de la tienda.	I asked them if I should bring them something from the store.

In requests or requirements, Spanish uses the conditional tense of the verb **querer**:

¿Querría usted sentarse?	Would you sit down?
¿Querrías pasarme la sal?	Would you pass me the salt?

The ***imperfecto*** is used in past contexts to refer to objects that "refuse" to work:

La puerta no se abría.	The door wouldn't open.
El lavavajillas no funcionaba.	The dishwasher wouldn't work.

The Spanish conditional tense can't be used in past contexts to refer to habitual actions. The ***imperfecto*** is used instead:

Él contaba chistes después de la cena.	He would tell jokes after dinner.

The ***imperfecto*** of the irregular verb ***soler*** is a good alternative:

Él solía contar chistes después de la cena.	He used to tell jokes after dinner.

Exercise 1

Fill in the blanks with the present, future, or future perfect tense of the verbs in parentheses. In some sentences more than one tense is possible.

1. Creo que el equipo griego _____ (ganar) el partido.

2. Esta noche _____ (nosotros cenar) con unos amigos.

3. ¿A qué hora _____ (salir) tu avión mañana?

4. Tengo una cita con el dentista. _____ (Yo tener) que estar en la consulta a las seis en punto.

5. Para el lunes que viene a estas horas, _____ (nosotros estar) disfrutando de unas bonitas vacaciones.

6. Para cuando volvamos el año que viene, _____ (ellos terminar) ya la nueva autopista.

7. Han tocado el timbre. _____ (ser) el cartero, pues
   _____ (él soler) venir a estas horas.

8. _____ (Yo querer) pasar unos días con mis abuelos la
   Navidad que viene.

Exercise 2
Underline the correct option. In some cases, both tenses are possible.

1. ¡Te *vas a arrepentir/arrepientes* de lo que me has hecho!

2. El parte meteorológico dice que mañana *llueve/va a llover* en el
   sur del país.

3. Mañana *habrá/hay* una reunión de jefes de sección. ¿Tú *vas/vas a
   ir*?

4. Si vienes después de las ocho, *empezaremos/vamos a empezar* a
   cenar sin ti.

5. Supongo que *había/ha habido* una fiesta salvaje, porque esta
   habitación está hecha un desastre.

6. No te *podré/puedo* recoger mañana a las siete, porque mi turno
   comienza/comenzará a las seis.

7. Si *apruebas/vas a aprobar* en junio, te *compraré/voy a comprar* la
   moto.

8. ¿A qué hora *tendrás/tienes* que recoger a Pablo del aeropuerto?

Exercise 3

Give advice or express criticism by means of conditional tenses as in the examples.

¡_____ *(Tú deber estudiar) más para el examen del lunes pasado!*
¡Deberías haber estudiado más para el examen del lunes pasado!
_____ *(Tú deber tener) más cuidado si no quieres tener otro*
accidente.
Deberías tener más cuidado si no quieres tener otro accidente.

1. Me _____ (tú poder echar) una mano con los

   ejercicios de ayer.

2. Si quieres adelgazar tanto, _____ (tú tener que

   empezar) primero por no comer tanto chocolate.

3. Pillaste ese resfriado porque ibas en mangas de camisa. Te

   _____ (tú deber poner) un abrigo.

4. ¿Todavía estás así? ¡Ya _____ (tú poder empezar)

   a pintar la cocina!

5. Llegué tarde porque tomé la salida equivocada.

   _____ (Yo tener que tomar) el primer desvío.

6. ¡Ya _____ (tú deber estar) lista! ¡Nos están

   esperando abajo!

7. _____ (Tú no deber hacer) tanto ruido. El bebé

   está durmiendo.

8. Te _____ (tú poder romper) el cuello cuando

   saltaste de esa forma.

9. No les _____ (tú deber decir) que estábamos en

casa.

10. Me _____ (tú poder recoger) un poco antes. Me

puse empapada.

The Subjunctive

Most of the verb forms that you have seen so far belong to the indicative mood. There are two other moods of verbs in Spanish: the subjunctive and the imperative.

In English, the subjunctive is the name of a special group of verb forms (*I be, she were*, etc.) which are used in a few cases to talk about events that are contrary to fact or are certain not to happen: you hope that they will happen, or imagine that they might happen, or you want them to happen:

If I were you, I wouldn't do that.
It is very important that he be invited.

The subjunctive is not very common today in English, and is often confined to formal language. English has other ways to express ideas of this kind. The Spanish subjunctive is extremely common; even Spanish-speaking children use it in their everyday conversations. It is impossible to avoid it.

Tense Explanations

The following explanations cover the subjunctive mood tense by tense. This is done to avoid confusion and to deal with important aspects that are related to time reference, degree of doubt, remote possibility, etc.

The Present Subjunctive

A structure like *I want him to come* is not possible to translate word-for-word in Spanish. When the speaker wants an action to be done by someone else, the conjunction *que* follows the verb in the main clause and the present subjunctive must be used in the subordinate clause:

Yo quiero que él coma con nosotros.	I want him to eat with us.
Te he dicho que (tú) no toques nada.	I have told you not to touch anything.
Ella me ha pedido que la ayude.	She has asked me to help her.

This means that English constructions of the type verb + object (pronoun or noun) + infinitive have to be translated by verb + *que* + subject of subordinate clause + subjunctive. If the sentence refers to the present or the future, the present tense of the subjunctive must be used:

Quiero que ellos estudien español.	I want them to study Spanish.
Necesito que María me ayude.	I need María to help me.
Yo te aconsejo que veas esa película.	I advise you to see that film.
Ella siempre nos dice que no fumemos.	She always tells us not to smoke.
Te he ordenado que limpies tu cuarto.	I have ordered you to clean your room.
No me gusta que él se ponga mi ropa.	I don't like him to put on my clothes./I don't like his putting on my clothes.

This subjunctive construction must also be used in Spanish when English uses the construction possessive/object pronoun + *-ing* form (*you/your going*):

Sugiero que compres ese coche.	I suggest your buying that car.
No me importa que fumes aquí.	I don't mind you/your smoking here.
No soporto que digas eso.	I can't stand you/your saying that.

The subjunctive also appears after *que* (*that*) in sentences in which the speaker expresses doubt, wish, possibility, probability, hypothesis, supposition, necessity, opinion, or uncertainty. The reference can be present and future:

No creo que él esté en casa.	I don't think (that) he is at home.
No creo que ella venga mañana.	I don't think that she will come tomorrow.
Es posible que él venda su casa.	It is possible that he will sell his house.
No es probable que llueva.	It is not probable that it will rain.
Espero que apruebes el examen.	I hope (that) you will pass the exam.
Sugiero que visites la torre.	I suggest that you visit the tower.

Ser + adjective + **que** and **estar** + adverb require subjunctive forms:

<u>*Es vital que*</u> *él esté aquí.*	It is vital that he be here.
<u>*Es bueno que*</u> *trabajes duro.*	It is good (a good thing) that you work hard.
No <u>*está bien que*</u> *bebas tanto.*	It isn't a good thing that you drink so much.

English often uses the modal verb *should* in constructions with the subjunctive. When this is the case, *should* is not translated. Spanish doesn't need auxiliaries in order to form the subjunctive:

No creo que Marcos deba estudiar aquí.	I don't think Marcos should study here.
Es vital que él sea tratado por un medico.	It's vital that he should be treated by a doctor.

The Spanish subjunctive preceded by **que** is very often the subject of a sentence. In English, this often has the form of possessive pronoun + -*ing* form (*his leaving*) at the beginning of a sentence:

<u>*Que ella tenga una fortuna*</u> *no es importante para mí.*	Her having a fortune is not important to me.

Que ellos nos ayuden con esto es lo <u>*que necesitamos.*</u>	Their helping us with this is what we need.

When **que** is preceded by the prepositions **sin, para, con, de**, and **según**, a subjunctive form must follow:

No debes hacer nada <u>sin que</u> yo <u>esté</u> *contigo.*	You shouldn't do anything without my being with you.
Estas lecciones son demasiado *difíciles <u>para que</u> él las entienda.*	These lessons are too difficult for him to understand.

Pretérito imperfecto

The **pretérito imperfecto** has two different forms in the subjunctive; both convey the same meaning and are interchangeable. The **pretérito imperfecto** of the subjunctive is used when the verb that appears before **que** is in a past tense and the sentence refers to that moment or to the future of that moment:

Ella no quiso que yo fuera con ella.	She didn't want me to go with her.
Ellos necesitaban que tú les *ayudaras.*	They needed you to help them.
Yo les sugerí que cogieran el tren.	I suggested their taking/that they should take the train.
Era posible que ella estuviera allí.	It was possible that she was there.
No era probable que ellos vinieran.	It wasn't probable that they would come.
No me importó que ella fumara.	I didn't mind her smoking.
Que yo aprobara en junio era pura *suerte.*	My passing in June was pure luck.

In the preceding examples, the other **imperfecto** form of the subjunctive (**fuese, ayudases, cogiesen**, etc.) can be used interchangeably.

The **pretérito imperfecto** of the subjunctive can be used in present contexts to refer to the present or to the future. The speaker then considers the possibility as remote or the style of communication as more polite:

Es posible que estuvieran aquí.	It's possible that they are here.

Es posible que estuvieran buscándonos.	It's possible that they are looking for us.
Quizás quisiera usted ayudarme.	Perhaps you could help me.

As you can see, the ***pretérito imperfecto*** of the subjunctive is often used in speculating about future or remote possibility and to express wishes:

Es posible que consiguieran vender la casa antes del lunes.	It is possible that they will manage to sell the house before Monday.
Si yo tuviera mucho dinero, yo me compraría un yate.	If I had a lot of money, I would buy a yacht.
Me gustaría que ella estuviera aquí más a menudo.	I would like her to be here more often.

In these sentences, the ***pretérito imperfecto*** of the subjunctive is often accompanied by conditional tenses.

Perfect Tenses of the Subjunctive

As you know, the verb ***haber*** is used with past participles to form perfect tenses. The present subjunctive of the verb ***haber*** and the corresponding past participle form the ***pretérito perfecto*** of the subjunctive, which is used to refer to the recent past. As with previous examples, the subjunctive follows the conjunction ***que***:

No creo que ella haya estado aquí.	I don't think that she has been here.
Es posible que él lo haya comprado.	It is possible that he has bought it.
No me gusta que hayas estado con ella.	I don't like (the idea of) your having been with her.
No está bien que le hayas pegado.	It isn't a good thing that you have hit him.

Many speakers in Latin America prefer using the ***pretérito imperfecto*** of the subjunctive instead of the ***pretérito perfecto*** (***haya estado***) in the preceding examples.

The *pretérito imperfecto* of the verb *haber* in the subjunctive plus a past participle form the *pretérito pluscuamperfecto* of the subjunctive. This tense is mainly used in conditional sentences (the "unreal" past) and to refer to actions that *had possibly taken place*:

Si hubieras/hubieses estado allí, habrías visto a la reina.	If you had been there, you would have seen the queen.
Yo no creía que ella hubiera estado allí.	I didn't believe that she had been there.

Summary and Specific Cases

As you have seen, the subjunctive usually appears in sentences in which the verb in the main clause deals with possibility, wanting, needing, ordering, requesting, etc., followed by *que* + subjunctive. The time reference of the subjunctive depends on the tense used in the main clause and, in some cases, on the possibility being remote or not. There are also certain verbs and constructions used in the negative that need to be followed by the subjunctive. What follows is an explanation of the general aspects of the subjunctive.

Present or Present Perfect + *Que* + Present Subjunctive

This structure can only refer to the present or to the future:

No creo que Juan tenga las llaves.	I don't think that Juan has the keys.
No creo que ella lo traiga.	I don't think that she will bring it.
No quiero que te pongas esa falda.	I don't want you to put on that skirt.

Examples with the *pretérito perfecto* follow:

Te he dicho que no llegues tarde.	I have told you not to be late.
Ella me ha ordenado que me vaya.	She has ordered me to leave.
Les hemos pedido que se queden.	We have asked them to stay.

Present Tense + *Que* + Imperfect Subjunctive

This structure usually refers to *that moment* in the past:

Yo no creo que ellos cogieran el dinero.	I don't think that they took the money.
Es probable que él les viera.	It's probable that he saw them.

The reference can also be to the future, but then the possibility is considered as remote or hypothetical:

Es posible que estuvieran aquí este lunes.	It's possible that they will be here next Monday.
No creo que él pudiera hacerlo mañana.	I don't think that he could do it tomorrow.

With the adjective ***posible*** and other words or expressions that denote doubt or possibility, the imperfect subjunctive can refer to the present:

Es posible que ellos estuvieran durmiendo.	It's possible that they are sleeping.
Es raro que ella supiera algo.	It's strange that she knows something.

Present Tense + *Que* + *Imperfecto/Perfecto/ Pluscuamperfecto* of the Subjunctive

If the past action expressed by the subjunctive is considered to be recent, the ***pretérito perfecto*** of the subjunctive is used:

No creo que ellos lo hayan visto.	I don't think that they have seen it.
Es posible que tú hayas aprobado.	It's possible that you have passed.

If the past action referred to is considered to be less recent, the ***pretérito imperfecto*** of the subjunctive must be used:

No creo que ella lo vendiera.	I don't think that she sold it.
Es probable que él los rompiera.	It's probable that he broke them.

The **pretérito pluscuamperfecto** of the subjunctive can also be used with the preceding examples, but there are some differences of meaning, depending on the context. In the sentence **Es posible que Juan los robara**, it is clear that the objects referred to were stolen (*It's possible that Juan stole them*). But **Es posible que Juan los hubiera robado** can mean that the objects referred to were not stolen. The speaker may be speculating about the possibility that John *would have* or *might have* stolen them if he had had the chance.

When the verbs in the main clause convey the idea of approval or disapproval, the **pretérito pluscuamperfecto** of the subjunctive usually implies that the action referred to did not take place. The sentence **No me importa que Marta lo hubiera usado** implies that Marta didn't use it, but I wouldn't have minded if she had. With these verbs, the **pretérito imperfecto** of the subjunctive usually refers to something that did, in fact, take place. If you say **No me importa que Marta lo usara**, it is clear that Marta did use it.

Past Tense + *Que* + *Imperfecto/Pluscuamperfecto* of the Subjunctive

In this construction, the imperfect subjunctive can refer to that moment in the past or to the future of that moment:

No quise que ella aprendiera a conducir.	I didn't want her to learn to drive.
Les dije que no usaran estos libros.	I told them not to use these books.
Era posible que él llegara ese día.	It was possible that he would arrive that day.
No creí que ella estuviera embarazada.	I didn't believe that she was pregnant.

If the reference is to a prior moment in the past, both the **imperfecto** and the **pluscuamperfecto** can usually be used:

No creí que ella dijera eso.	I didn't believe that she said (had said) that.
No creí que ella hubiera dicho eso.	

Me sorprendió que mi hijo hiciera eso.	It surprised me that my son did (had done) that.
Me sorprendió que mi hijo hubiera hecho eso.	

With compound tenses that use the verb **estar**, only the **pluscuamperfecto** can refer to a prior moment in the past:

Me extrañó que ella hubiera estado embarazada.	It amazed me that she had been pregnant.

In some cases, the meaning of the sentence depends on which past tense is used in the main clause. **Yo querría que ella viniera** can mean that she hadn't come yet. **Yo quise que ella viniera** means that she had already come. **No me importaba que él comiera con nosotros** refers to that moment or to the future of that moment. **No me importó que él comiera con nosotros** can only mean that he had already eaten with us.

Verbs that Denote Opinion and Reported Speech

Most of the verbs that denote opinion are only followed by subjunctive forms when they are negative:

Creo que ella está enferma.	I think that she is ill.
No creo que ella esté enferma.	I don't think that she is ill.
Me parece que él es médico.	It seems to me that he is a doctor.
No me parece que él sea médico.	It doesn't seem to me that he is a doctor.

Verbs that denote reported speech (**decir**, **comentar**, **contar**, etc.) can be followed by both subjunctive and indicative forms when they are negative and without significant differences of meaning:

Yo no he dicho que ella haya cogido/ha cogido el dinero.	I haven't said that she has taken the money.
Ella no comentó que él estuviera/ estaba casado.	She didn't comment that he was married.

The Future Tense of the Subjunctive

The future tense of the subjunctive is confined to extremely formal language, such as that found in laws, contracts, and other documents. It is not in common use and this book does not address the issue.

Variation of *Haber*

As you know, *there is* and *there are* both mean **hay**, and *there was* and *there were* mean **había** or **hubo**. The infinitive of these forms is **haber**. This means that the verb **haber** has two functions; one is to conjugate perfect tenses (**yo he comido, tú has venido**, etc.) and the other is to translate the expressions described previously (*there is, there are*, etc.). The subjunctive form of **hay** is **haya**; remember, there is no subject in Spanish and the same word is used for both singular and plural. The subjunctive form of **había** is **hubiera** or **hubiese** (both forms are correct). There is no corresponding subjunctive form for the **pretérito indefinido** (**hubo**). The use of the subjunctive of **haber** corresponds to the same expressions that deal with doubt, wishes, possibility, necessity, uncertainty, etc.:

No creo que haya problemas esta noche.	I don't think that <u>there will be</u> problems tonight. (*future reference*)
No creo que haya leche en la cocina.	I don't think that <u>there is</u> milk in the kitchen. (*reference to the present*)
Es posible que hubiera problemas.	It's possible that <u>there were some</u> problems. (*reference to the past*)
Es posible que vaya a haber problemas.	It's possible that <u>there will be</u> some problems. (*future reference with some degree of uncertainty*)
Es posible que haya problemas.	It's possible that <u>there are</u> some problems. (*present reference with some uncertainty*)

As you can see, the imperfect subjunctive depends on the context when *es posible/probable* is used. If the verb in the main clause (the part before *que*) is in the past, the imperfect subjunctive can refer to that moment or to a future moment in the past:

Era posible que hubiera más personas en la casa en aquel <u>momento</u>.	It's possible that there were more people in the house <u>at that moment</u>.
Era posible que hubiera tormenta <u>a la mañana siguiente</u>.	It was possible that there would be a storm <u>the following morning</u>.

The past participle of *haber* is *habido*. If you use the subjunctive forms of the auxiliary verb *haber* with this past participle, you form the perfect tenses of the subjunctive: *haya habido* (*there has/have been*), *hubiera/hubiese habido* (*there had been*):

No creo que <u>haya habido</u> un accidente.	I don't think that there has been an accident.

Latin Americans prefer the *imperfecto*:

No creo que hubiera un accidente.	I don't think that there was/there has been an accident.

Similarly to English, past perfect tenses refer to a prior moment in the past:

Es posible que hubiera habido más gente.	It's possible that there had been more people.
No creo que hubiera habido un terremoto.	I don't think that there had been an earthquake.

Exercise 1
Underline the correct option.

1. Te he dicho que no *toques/tocas* nada sin mi permiso.

2. Recuerdo que ella *dijo/dijera* algo así.

3. Estoy deseando que *termina/termine* el colegio.

4. Creo que Juan *tiene/tenga* uno igual en su casa.

5. Ella ha dicho que su hijo *va/vaya* a suspender.

6. No te dije que *vinieras/viniste* tan temprano.

7. Le pedí a la cajera que lo *comprobase/comprobaba* otra vez.

8. Sugiero que *alquilamos/alquilemos* una película.

9. He oído que te *has/hayas* casado.

10. Te advierto que no *tengo/tenga* ese dinero.

Exercise 2
Correct any mistakes.

1. Les advertí que no se acercaban al borde.

_____

2. ¿Es seguro que vengan a las siete?

_____

3. Me parece que vamos a tener tormenta.

_____

4. Si yo había sabido eso, no habría ido allí.

_____

5. Es muy importante que terminemos esto hoy.

_____

6. Que él sea culpable está cada vez más claro.

_____

7. Que él sea elegido es lo más importante.

_____

8. No fue necesario que les avisáramos.

_____

9. ¡Que te estás quieto, hombre!

_____

10. Creo que ella sabe hacerlo, pero no creo que quiera.

_____

Exercise 3

Fill in the blanks with an appropriate tense of the verbs in parentheses.

Mi prima Lara me _____ (llamar) el otro día. _____ (Querer)

que yo _____ (hablar) con mi amigo Miguel y le _____

(preguntar) si ella le _____ (gustar). Al principio no me

_____ (parecer) una buena idea, pero después de un rato de

conversación, _____ (conseguir) convencerme. Así que, después de

_____ (colgar) el teléfono, _____ (marcar) el número de

Miguel. No lo _____ (coger). _____ (Pensar) que _____

(ir) al gimnasio, ya que él _____ (entrenar) mucho últimamente.

_____ (Decidir) ir a buscarle. Cuando _____ (llegar) me

dijeron que ya se _____ (marchar) y que le _____ (buscar) en el bar de su tío, porque era probable que _____ (estar) allí. Al

_____ (llegar) al bar, vi cómo Miguel y una espléndida rubia se

_____ (hacer) mimos _____ (sentar) a una mesa en un

rincón. _____ (Comprender) que no _____ (tener) sentido

que le _____ (molestar) en un momento como ése y, _____

(aprovechar) que aún no me _____ (ver), me _____ (ir) a mi

casa.

The Imperative

You may have noticed that imperative forms are, in fact, subjunctive forms except with affirmative forms of *tú* and *vosotros*. In the negative, *tú* and *vosotros* have subjunctive forms:

Come.	Eat.
No comas.	Don't eat.
Hablad (vosotros).	Talk.
No hables (tú).	Don't talk.

Subject pronouns with imperatives usually have an emphatic or clarifying purpose and can easily be omitted. When they are used, they usually come after the imperative form. Remember that *usted* and *ustedes* always go with third-person forms:

No vengáis vosotros.	Don't come.
Pase usted.	Come in.

The imperative normally refers to the person(s) spoken to:

Limpia el suelo.	Clean the floor.
Hable más despacio, por favor.	Speak slower, please.
Hablad (vosotros) inglés.	Speak English.

It has become customary to use infinitive forms as imperatives in street signs, public notices, and warnings. This is often done when the audience is the general public:

No pisar el césped.	Keep off the grass.
No traspasar.	Don't trespass.

As a result of this, many Spaniards use infinitives with ***vosotros*** instead of true imperatives in everyday speech, but this is not considered correct. Remember that the ***vosotros*** form is used throughout Spain. Many Latin Americans use ***ustedes*** instead.

The imperative form with ***nosotros*** is equivalent to constructions with *let's* in English:

Cojamos el autobús.	Let's take the bus.
Comamos en el jardín.	Let's eat in the garden.
Veamos.	Let's see.

The imperative first-person plural form of the verb ***ir*** (*to go*) is ***vayamos***, but the form ***vamos*** is usually used when making suggestions:

Vamos a la playa.	Let's go to the beach.

Third-person imperative forms must be preceded by the conjunction ***que***. These forms are like the English expression *let/make someone do something* and can be used with pronouns or nouns:

Que pasen.	Let them come in./Make them come in.
Que coman ellos primero.	Let them eat first.
Que pase la niña.	Let the girl come in.
Que coma María primero.	Let María eat first.

The word ***que*** is not used in sentences like *¡**Viva el rey!*** (*Long live the king!*)

Subject pronouns with imperatives are used to clarify who the imperative refers to:

Que pase él, no ella.	Let him come in, not her.

Que is often used to express imperatives with a greater sense of urgency. When this is the case, only subjunctive forms are possible. This sense of urgency can be used with ***tú***, ***vosotros***, ***usted***, and ***ustedes***:

¡Estudiad!	Study!
¡Que estudiéis!	Study!

As you already know, many Spanish verbs are conjugated by means of reflexive pronouns. This is done to indicate to whom the action of the verb refers or whom the direct object is for. In the imperative, the use of these pronouns is equally usual:

Bébete la leche.	Drink up your milk.
Vístanse rápidamente.	Get dressed quickly.

In the preceding examples (both affirmative commands), the reflexive pronoun always comes after the verb and is attached to it. With affirmative **nosotros** commands, the final **-s** of the verb is dropped before adding the reflexive pronoun. Compare:

Comamos.	Let's eat.
Comámonos eso.	Let's eat that.

With affirmative **vosotros** commands, reflexive verbs drop the **d.** The only exception to this occurs with the verb **ir**, although in conversation **iros** is more common:

¡Callaos (vosotros)!	Be quiet!
Lavaos el pelo.	Wash your hair.

If the imperative is negative, the reflexive pronoun must come before the verb:

No te comas eso.	Don't eat that.
No nos sentemos aquí.	Let's not sit down here.
No os levantéis.	Don't get up.

When **que** is used in the imperative, the reflexive pronoun must come before the verb as well:

¡Que te comas eso!	Eat that!
¡Que te vayas!	Leave!
Que se acuesten temprano.	Let them go to bed early.

The imperatives of transitive verbs (i.e., verbs that can take a direct object) attach the indirect object pronoun (the person who receives the object) plus the direct object pronoun (the object being received) to the imperative form:

Dámelo.	Give it to me.
Dánoslos.	Give them to us.

Actions referring to third persons (*he, she, it,* and *they*) always use the pronoun *se*:

Dáselo.	Give it to him/her/them.

The pronouns *lo*, *la*, *los*, and *las* must agree in number and gender with the object referred to by the pronoun:

Dámelas.	Give them to me.

If the imperative is negative, the pronouns go before the verb:

No se las des.	Don't give them to him/her/them.

In some cases, certain English verbs omit the pronoun *it* when talking about what has happened before:

Antonio: Do you know what happened?
Bernardo: No, tell me, please. (*it* omitted)

In Spanish, *lo* must always be used in these cases:

A: *¿Sabes lo que pasó?*
B: *No, dímelo, por favor.*

Exercise 1

Make imperative constructions of the following sentences, as in the examples.

Tú no debes tocar eso.
No toques eso.
Juan debe ayudarte con los deberes.
Que te ayude Juan./Que Juan te ayude con los deberes.

1. La pequeña no debe ver esa película.

2. Tú no debes enviárselo.

3. Marco debe lavar los platos esta vez.

4. Tú no tienes que pagarnos nada.

5. Debes prestarme el coche esta noche.

6. No quiero que se lo traigas mañana.

7. Necesito que se lo traigas esta noche.

8. Usted no debe entrar sin mi permiso.

9. Tú tienes que estudiar para aprobar ese examen.

_____

10. Nosotros debemos irnos ya.

_____

Exercise 2
Correct any mistakes.

1. Que no vete todavía.

_____

2. Dálese a Elena esta tarde.

_____

3. Hagámonos unos bocadillos.

_____

4. Pongámosnos aquí.

_____

5. Se tumbe la niña en el sofá.

_____

6. Ayúdame usted, por favor.

_____

7. Llévaselas a su dormitorio.

_____

Translating English Modal Verbs

Spanish doesn't have modal verbs. Some of the English modals (for example, *can*, *may*, or *must*) are independent verbs in Spanish. Other English modals are actually conjugation endings, like the future tense: *yo comeré* (*I will eat*). In order to make a reasonable comparison, English modal verbs are explained individually.

Can/Could (Ability/Possibility)

When saying what the subject of the sentence is able to do, and when talking about possibility, the irregular verb *poder* is used:

Ella puede levantar 100 kilos.	She can lift 100 kilos.
Ellos pueden correr muy deprisa.	They can run very fast.
Yo no puedo venir mañana.	I can't come tomorrow.
Ese perro puede ser peligroso.	That dog can be dangerous.
Ella no puede levantarse.	She can't get up.
Ellos no pudieron entrar.	They couldn't get in.
Juan no pudo coger el avión.	Juan couldn't take the plane.

When the ability is the result of a learning process (*I can swim, she can speak five languages, he can't play the guitar*), the irregular verb *saber* is used instead:

Ella sabe cocinar muy bien.	She can cook very well.
Pepe sabe tocar el piano.	Pepe can play the piano.
Yo no sé hablar ruso.	I can't speak Russian.
Él sabía jugar a las cartas muy bien.	He could play cards very well.

Remember that the *imperfecto* refers to a more or less habitual situation in the past, while the *pretérito indefinido* refers to an action at a certain moment in the past.

It is not always easy to explain when to use *saber* instead of *poder*. There are even cases in which both verbs are possible, but usually with a difference of meaning. *María sabe montar en bicicleta* (*María can ride a bike*) means that María has learned how to do it. *María puede montar en bici* means that she is able to do it despite something (perhaps she is not in good physical condition). It can even mean that she is allowed to ride a bike. When *poder* is used in this type of context, the person referred to already knows how to perform the action.

When the context refers to the past, *poder* is used in the *imperfecto* or the *pretérito indefinido.* If the context refers to the future or to a hypothetical present, Spanish uses *poder* in the conditional:

Podríamos ser ricos.	We could be rich.
Si fueras allí, podrías aprender inglés.	If you went there, you could learn English.

Because the modal verb *can* doesn't have a past participle and can't be used with other modal verbs, English speakers have to use the verb *to be able to* instead. The verb *poder* can be conjugated in all tenses:

No he podido encontrarlo.	I haven't been able to find it.
No podremos hacerlo.	We won't be able to do it.
Ayer pude conseguir las entradas.	I was able to get the tickets yesterday.

Can/Could/May/Might (Permission)

These four verbs are translated by different tenses of *poder* when the speaker is asking for permission or granting permission:

¿Puedo usar tu bolígrafo?	Can I use your pen?
¿Puedo aparcar aquí?	May/Can I park here?

In English, the degree of formality is achieved by choosing one modal verb or another (*can* or *may*, for example), but in Spanish it is achieved by using formal subject pronouns in the course of the conversation (***usted*** and ***ustedes***), as well as possessive pronouns that correspond to ***usted*** and ***ustedes***. Remember, these pronouns take the third-person form:

¿Puedo usar su teléfono?	May I use your telephone?

In asking for permission, *could* and *might* are translated by the conditional tense of the verb ***poder***. In Spanish, this tense is used to express politeness:

¿Podría usar su teléfono, por favor?	Could I use your phone, please?

As in English, the conditional is never used to give permission. The imperative of the verb that was used in the question is usual:

Sí, úsalo. (tú)	Yes, use it.
Sí, úselo. (usted)	

The present tense of ***poder*** is another way to answer this type of question. It is often accompanied by a second *sí*:

Sí, sí puedes.	Yes, you can.

Sometimes no verb is used:

Sí, por supuesto.	Yes, of course/certainly.

These possibilities can be used together:

Sí, por supuesto, úselo.
Sí, por supuesto, puede usarlo.

The imperative of the verb ***hacer*** and the object pronoun ***lo*** are often used as a general answer:

¿Puedo quedarme aquí?	Can I stay here?
Sí, hazlo.	Yes, do it. (*literal translation*)

If the answer is negative, there are many possibilities, depending on the verb used in the question:

No, no puedes.   No, you can't.
No, lo siento, no puedes.   No, I'm sorry, you can't.
Lo siento, lo voy a necesitar.   I'm sorry, I'm going to need it.

Can/Could (Asking to Do Things)

The present and the conditional of *poder* are used to ask someone to do things. The conditional is slightly more polite, although politeness in general will always depend on the speaker's tone and the use of the pronouns *usted* and *ustedes*:

¿Podría usted sujetar esto, por favor?   Could you hold this, please?

¿Puedes ayudarme con este ejercicio?   Can you help me with this exercise?

Could translates as *podría*, *podrías*, etc. (conditional tense) in direct speech. In reported speech, *could* can be translated as *podía*, *podías*, etc. (imperfect tense) when the direct question was asked by means of the present, and as the conditional (*podría*, *podrías*, etc.) if the question was asked in the conditional:

¿Puede usted prestarme su coche? (direct speech)   Can you lend me your car?

Ella me preguntó si yo podía prestarle mi coche. (reported speech)   She asked me if I could lend her my car.

¿Podrías ayudarme con mis ejercicios? (direct speech)   Could you help me with my exercises?

Ella me preguntó si yo podría ayudarla con sus ejercicios. (reported speech)   She asked me if I could help her with her exercises.

May/Might/Could (Possibility/Doubt)

In this case, all three verbs are translated as *puede que* followed by a subject and a subjunctive form. *Puede que* is invariable:

Puede que ella esté en casa.	She may/might/could be at home.
Puede que ellos vengan mañana.	They may/might/could come tomorrow.
Puede que Pedro tenga los documentos.	Pedro may/might/could have the documents.

Puede que doesn't give any information about the degree of doubt. The present subjunctive form refers to the present or to the future (the context will make this clear):

Puede que ellos estén trabajando ahora.	They may be working now.
Puede que ellos aprueben en junio.	They may pass in June.

Past subjunctive forms usually refer to the past:

Puede que ellos cogieran el dinero.	They may/might have taken the money.

Past subjunctive forms can also be used to refer to the present or to the future, but then the possibility is considered to be remote:

Puede que ella estuviera en casa ahora.	She might/could be at home now.
Puede que vinieran mañana.	They might come tomorrow.

To refer to the past, English uses *may have* or *might have* and a past participle (*He may/might have done it.*). Spanish uses either the past subjunctive or the present subjunctive of the verb **haber** (*have*) and a past participle. The difference hinges on what the speaker considers recent:

Puede que él haya visto el accidente.	He may/might have seen the accident.
Puede que él viera el accidente.	He may/might have seen the accident.

In the first sentence, the speaker considers that the accident happened recently. In the second sentence, the speaker places the accident further back in the past. You might want to review the differences between the **pretérito indefinido** and the **pretérito perfecto** in Chapters 9 and 11. The perfect tenses are common usage in Spain. Latin Americans rarely use them, since they prefer the simple past tenses whether the action is recent or not.

When the context makes it very clear that the sentence is expressing possibility or doubt, the construction is the same as in English:

Ellos pueden venir mañana.	They may come tomorrow.
Ella puede estar enferma.	She may be ill.

With **podría**, which expresses a more remote possibility, the infinitive follows:

Ella podría comprarlo mañana.	She could buy it tomorrow.
Ellos podrían estar en casa.	They could be at home.
Ellos podrían haber estado en casa.	They could have been at home.

In these sentences, the **imperfecto** of **poder** is often used, especially when possibilities are being discussed and when the speaker's tone denotes a certain degree of irritation:

¡Podías echarme una mano!	You could lend me a hand!

The construction **podría ser que** is followed by the past subjunctive to refer to the present, past, or future, or by a past perfect subjunctive to refer only to past actions:

Podría ser que aprobaras en junio.	You could pass in June.
Podría ser que estuvieras embarazada.	You might/could be pregnant.
Podría ser que ellos comieran aquí ayer.	They might/could have eaten here yesterday.
Podría ser que hubieran comido aquí.	They might/could have eaten here.

Comieran aquí and **hubieran comido aquí** are interchangeable in these examples.

Puede ser que expresses a less remote possibility or doubt. It can be followed by present and past subjunctive forms to refer to different time contexts:

Puede ser que estén en casa.	They may be at home.
Puede ser que estuvieran en casa.	They might be at home.
Puede ser que estuvieran en casa ayer.	They might have been at home yesterday.
Puede ser que hayan estado en casa hoy.	They may/might have been at home today.
Puede ser que hubieran estado allí ayer.	They might have been there yesterday.

Must/to Have to

The verb *must* is translated by **deber**, and *to have to* by **tener que**. Both verbs are used to express obligation:

Debes estar aquí a las diez.	You must be here at ten.
Ella tiene que limpiar esto.	She has to clean this.

As in English, they are not equivalent when the sentence is negative. **No deber** is an obligation not to do something; **no tener que** expresses lack of obligation to do something:

No debes fumar en clase.	You mustn't smoke in class.
No tengo que trabajar mañana.	I don't have to work tomorrow.

In English, the verb *must* is used when the speaker expresses his or her conviction, and the verb *to have to* is used when the obligation is not connected with the speaker's authority or conviction. In Spanish, this difference is not as clear. Both verbs have similar uses in affirmative sentences, and **tener que** can appear in sentences in which English only uses *must*. **Tener que** is much more common in conversational Spanish than **deber**:

Tengo que recoger a los niños.	I have to pick up the children.
Tienes que estudiar más.	You must/have to study harder.
¡Tienes que hacerlo!	You must do it!

In the negative, the verb ***deber*** is used to express obligation not to do something:

No debes pegar a tus compañeros.	You mustn't hit your fellow students.
Ella no debe saber esto.	She mustn't know this.
Ellos no deben usar los ordenadores.	They mustn't use the computers.

In negative sentences, ***no tener que*** implies that the speaker doesn't have an obligation to do something:

No tengo que recoger a Tom.	I don't have to pick up Tom.
Ellos no tienen que ir al colegio.	They don't have to go to school.

Sometimes ***no tener que*** can mean the same as *shouldn't*, especially when the speaker expresses anger or reproach:

¡No tienes que fumar!	You shouldn't smoke!

The construction ***no tener por qué*** is often used instead of ***no tener que***, but there is usually a difference of meaning. ***No tener por qué*** implies that the speaker can choose not to do something if he doesn't want to:

No tengo que levantarme temprano mañana.	I don't have to get up early tomorrow.
No tengo por qué levantarme temprano mañana.	I don't have to get up early tomorrow.

The first example expresses that I don't have an obligation to get up early, perhaps because I am on vacation. The second example very clearly expresses that I can choose to get up later if I want to. In other words, ***no tener por qué*** conveys the idea of *there is no reason why I should do it.*

The ***imperfecto*** of the verb ***deber*** refers to past obligations known in advance:

Él me dijo que yo <u>debía/tenía que</u> estar allí a las diez en punto.	He told me that I must/had to be there at ten o'clock.

Mi padre me dijo que yo <u>no debía</u> usar su coche.	My father told me that I mustn't use his car.
Debía estar allí a las diez.	I had to be there at ten.

The **pretérito indefinido** of **deber** is used in the affirmative to refer to actions in the past that should have been done, but that the subject didn't do. In the negative, it expresses something that should not have been done. English expresses this with constructions of the type *should have* + past participle. In other words, the **pretérito indefinido** of the verb **deber** usually implies reproach, while the **pretérito indefinido** of the verb **tener que** can refer to both obligation and reproach. Compare:

Debí estar allí a las diez.	I should have been there at ten. (*but I wasn't*)
Debí estudiar más.	I should have studied harder. (*but I didn't*)
Tuve que venderlo.	I had to sell it.
No tuviste que hacer eso.	You shouldn't have done that.

Perfect tenses (with the auxiliary verb **haber**) express certain nuances. If the verb **deber** is used, the sentence implies reproach, not obligation:

Has debido hacerlo.	You should have done it.
Has debido hablar con él.	You should have talked to him.
No has debido comprar eso.	You shouldn't have bought that.

Perfect tenses of **tener que** don't usually convey reproach, but the construction **tener que** (in the imperfect) + **haber** + past participle can only be used to refer to something that should or should not have been done:

He tenido que hacerlo.	I've had to do it. (*obligation*)
Tenía que haber estudiado más.	I should have studied harder. (*reproach*)

Spanish speakers in Latin America prefer the simple tenses to the perfect ones. This means that the sentences **Has debido hacerlo** and **He tenido que hacerlo** become **Debiste hacerlo** and **Tuve que hacerlo**, without regard to how recently the action took place. But the construction *tener que* (in the imperfect) + *haber* + past participle, which implies reproach instead of obligation, is used by all Spanish speakers.

The verb *must* does not have a future tense in English, but the future tense of *deber* is quite common in Spanish, even though the future of *tener que* is usually heard more in casual conversations:

Deberemos estar allí a las once.	We will have to be there at eleven o'clock.
Tendremos que estar allí a las once.	
Ellos deberán comportarse.	They will have to behave.
Ellos tendrán que comportarse.	

In negative sentences, the future tense of *deber* implies an obligation not to do something in the future, but expressed with a certain degree of uncertainty. *Deber* in the future can also be a simple prediction. As such, it is usually translated as *must not* or *should not*. The negative future tense of *tener que* corresponds to *won't have to*:

No deberemos hablar con él.	We must not/shouldn't talk to him.
No tendremos que hablar con él.	We won't have to talk to him.

When in doubt, use the present tense of the indicative mood of the verb *deber* to refer to the future:

Mañana vamos a la reunión, pero no debemos mencionar esto.	We are going to the meeting tomorrow, but we shouldn't mention this.

As in English, the verb *deber* plus the preposition *de* is also used to express deductions, although many Spanish speakers omit *de* when using this expression:

Deben de ser las seis.	It must be six o'clock.
Deben ser las seis.	
Debes de estar muy cansado.	You must be very tired.

Remember that *deber* by itself shows obligation; with *de* it shows deduction. Compare:

Debes tener 18 años para entrar en una discoteca.	You must be 18 years old to enter a disco. (*obligation*)
No sé tu edad, pero debes de tener unos 18 años.	I don't know your age, but you must be about 18. (*deduction*)

Tener que can also be used to express deductions:

No sé tu edad, pero tienes que tener unos 18 años.	I don't know your age, but you must be about 18.
Tienen que ser las seis.	It must be six o'clock.

When the verb **tener que** is used this way, the speaker shows a higher degree of conviction than when the verb **deber** is used.

Negative deductions in English are expressed by the verb *can't* (or *couldn't*). In Spanish, **no deber de**, **no tener que**, and **no poder** can be used without significant differences:

Ese hombre no debe de ser muy rico.	That man can't be very rich.
Ese hombre no tiene que ser muy rico.	
Ese hombre no puede ser muy rico.	

Both positive and negative deductions in the past are expressed by simply conjugating the past simple tenses of these verbs. Unlike English, Spanish doesn't need to use the verb **haber** in order to refer to deductions made in the past:

Sara comentó que yo debía de/ tenía que tener 40 años.	Sara commented that I must have been 40 years old.
Eso debió de/tuvo que costarte una fortuna.	That must have cost you a fortune.
Ese hombre no podía/no debía de/ no tenía que estar muerto, ya que yo le había visto en un restaurante aquella mañana.	That man can't have been dead, as I had seen him in a restaurant that morning.

In deductions, the **imperfecto** refers to that moment in the past. The **pretérito indefinido** refers to completed actions:

Ellos debían de estar casados.	They must have been married (then).
Eso debió de ocurrir antes.	That must have happened before.

Perfect tenses are possible when there is a certain sense of recentness:

Eso ha debido de ser muy duro para ti.	That must have been very hard for you.
Eso ha tenido que ser muy duro para ti.	

Instead of using past tenses of the verbs ***deber de*** and ***tener que***, the construction ***deber de/tener que*** + ***haber*** + past participle can be used in the present tense:

Eso debe de haber sido muy duro para ti.	That must have been very hard for you.
Eso tiene que haber sido muy duro para ti.	

In fact, the construction ***deber de*** + ***haber*** + past participle is really the literal translation of *must have* + past participle, but Spanish only uses it when it refers to something recent.

Needn't

This modal verb translates as ***no hace falta que*** or ***no es necesario que***. Both forms are followed by present subjunctive forms:

No hace falta que vengas.	You needn't come.
No es necesario que vengas.	
No hace falta que traigas nada.	You needn't bring anything.
No es necesario que traigas nada.	

Because the negative form of *have to* has the same meaning, *needn't* can also be translated as ***no tener que***:

No tienes que venir mañana.	You needn't come tomorrow.

No tienes que hacer las camas.	You needn't make the beds.

No tener por qué + infinitive is usually used to emphasize that the subject can choose to do or not do the action. The decision does not depend on anyone or anything else:

No tienes por qué venir mañana.	You needn't come tomorrow.
No tienes por qué hacer las camas.	You needn't make the beds.
No tienes por qué darme dinero.	You needn't give me money.

In English, the past of *needn't* is *didn't have to* or *didn't need to*. In Spanish, the **imperfecto** of the verbs **tener**, **hacer**, and **ser** is used:

Ella no tenía que trabajar ese sábado.	She didn't have to work that Saturday.
Ellos no tenían que hacerlo.	They didn't have/need to do it.
No hacía falta que ella viniera.	She didn't have/need to come.
No era necesario que yo les ayudara.	I didn't have/need to help them.

In English, *didn't have to* implies that the action was not done because the subject was not obliged to do it. In Spanish, this is generally shown by using either the **imperfecto** or the **pretérito indefinido**. If the **imperfecto** is used, it isn't clear whether the action was done or not. It can convey the idea that the action was done despite the fact that the subject was not obliged to do it, or it can imply that the action was not done because the subject knew in advance that he or she wasn't obliged to do it. The context usually makes this understood. If the **pretérito indefinido** is used, then it is clear that the action was not done. Compare the following examples:

Aunque no hacía falta que ella me ayudara, ella vino e hizo las camas.	Although it wasn't necessary for her to help me, she came and made the beds.
Ella no vino, porque yo le dije que no hacía falta que viniera.	She didn't come because I told her that it wasn't necessary for her to come.
No hizo falta que yo le ayudara; él ya lo había terminado.	I didn't have to help him; he had already finished it.

Aunque yo no tenía que trabajar ese sábado, fui a la oficina a ayudar a mis colegas.	Although I wasn't obliged to work that Saturday, I went to the office to help my colleagues.
Cuando llegamos, no tuvimos que rescatar a nadie.	When we arrived, we didn't have to rescue anybody.

The differences in English between *needn't* and *don't need to* (the verb *to need* is **necesitar**) correspond to Spanish usage:

No necesitas tener un visado.	You don't need to have a visa.
No tienes por qué quedarte.	You needn't stay.

When an unnecessary action has taken place, English uses *needn't have* + past participle. Spanish uses the *imperfecto* of **no tener que** + **haber** + past participle:

No tenías que haber venido.	You needn't have come.
No tenías que haberme traído nada.	You needn't have brought me anything.

The same idea can be translated by means of the *imperfecto* of **tener que**, **no hacer falta**, and **no ser necesario que** (the last two always followed by past tenses of the subjunctive). Remember that the imperfect tense often implies that the action was done despite the lack of obligation:

No tenías que comprar nada.	You needn't have bought anything.
No tenías por qué comprar nada.	You needn't have bought anything.
No hacía falta que compraras nada.	You needn't have bought anything.
No era necesario que compraras nada.	You needn't have bought anything.
No tenías que haber comprado nada.	You needn't have bought anything.

Should/Ought to/Had Better

These three verbs can all be translated by the conditional tense of ***deber***:

Deberías comer menos.	You should eat less.
	You ought to eat less.
	You'd better eat less.
No deberías fumar delante del bebé.	You shouldn't smoke in front of the baby.
	You oughtn't smoke . . .
	You'd better not smoke . . .

Because *ought to* is usually used in more formal contexts, it can also be translated by the present tense of the verb ***deber***, depending on the speaker's tone and intentions.

The modal construction *had better* can also be translated by the construction ***ser*** (in the conditional) + ***mejor que***, always followed by the past subjunctive:

Sería mejor que cogieras un taxi.	You'd better take a taxi.
Sería mejor que no hablaras con ella.	You'd better not talk with her.

The verb ***ser*** in this construction has no subject and it is always in the singular.

To create similar meanings to those in English, add the infinitive ***haber*** and past participle to the conditional ***debería***, or use the verbs ***deber*** and ***tener que*** in the ***pretérito indefinido***:

Deberías haber cogido el dinero.	You should have taken the money.
No deberías haber hecho eso.	You shouldn't have done that.
Debiste coger el dinero.	You should have taken the money.
No debiste hacer eso.	You shouldn't have done that.

Note: The construction ***ser mejor que*** can't be used this way.

As in English, the conditional form ***debería*** can be used to give advice, to make suggestions and, when accompanied by the verb ***haber***, to reproach or censure someone's actions. The construction **ser mejor que** can't be used to reproach or censure actions:

No deberías beber tanto.	You shouldn't drink so much.
Deberías haber hecho tus deberes.	You should have done your homework.
Deberíamos comer en ese restaurante.	We should/We'd better eat in that restaurant.

Remember that the construction **tener que** + **haber** + past participle can also be used in reproaching or censuring someone's actions:

| *No tenías que haber pagado.* | You shouldn't have paid. |
| *Tenías que haber venido antes.* | You should have come before. |

It is even possible to use the **pretérito indefinido** of **tener que** or **deber**:

| *No tuviste que/debiste pagar.* | You shouldn't have paid. |
| *Tuviste que/Debiste dejarles entrar.* | You should have let them come in. |

Tener que usually depends on the context when used in these types of sentences:

| *Veo que has lavado los platos, pero no tenías que haberlo hecho, ya que tenemos lavavajillas.* | I see that you have washed the dishes, but you needn't have done it, since we have a dishwasher. |
| *No tenías que haberles dicho nada/ No tuviste que decirles nada/No debiste decirles nada; ahora conocen nuestro secreto.* | You shouldn't have told them anything; now they know our secret. |

Would Rather

This modal combination is translated as **preferiría** (the conditional tense of **preferir**):

Yo preferiría comprar el otro.   I'd rather buy the other one.
Ella preferiría casarse contigo.   She'd rather get married to you.

When ***preferiría*** isn't followed by an infinitive, it is followed by ***que*** + the subjunctive in the past tense:

Yo preferiría que no vinieras.   I'd rather you didn't come.
Ella preferiría que te quedaras.   She'd rather you stayed.

Preferiría can be used with nouns and pronouns:

Yo preferiría un café.   I would prefer a coffee.
Ella preferiría un buen libro.   She would prefer a good book.

The modal verbs *shall, will,* and *would* have already been covered in their corresponding chapters.

Exercise 1

Rewrite the following sentences as in the examples.

Deduzco que esa chica es alemana.
Esa chica debe de ser alemana.
Es posible que mis padres vendan la casa.
Puede que mis padres vendan la casa.

1. ¡Cállate!

¿——————————————————————————

2. No creo que las tiendas estén abiertas.

Las tiendas ——————————————————————

3. Me parece imposible que Luisa se haya casado.

Luisa no ——————————————————————

4. Deberías ir al dentista.

Sería ——————————————————————

5. Es posible que vengan esta noche.

Podría _____

6. Me ha sido imposible terminar el trabajo.

No he _____

7. ¿Necesitas ayuda mañana?

¿Te hace _____

8. Estuvo muy mal que les insultaras.

No les _____

9. No era necesario que trajeras tanta cerveza.

No _____

10. En Inglaterra no puedes conducir por la derecha.

En Inglaterra _____

Exercise 2

Five of the following sentences contain errors. Correct them.

1. Si yo tuviera más dinero, no viviría en este barrio.

_____

2. Yo preferiría que ella esté aquí más a menudo.

_____

3. Ahora no tengo nada que hacer. ¿Te echaré una mano?

_____

4. Puede ser que haya extraterrestres en el gobierno.

_____

5. Ya deben de ser las once.

_____

6. Sería mejor que no hubieras hecho eso.

_____

7. Puede que ellos cenan con nosotros mañana.

_____

8. No hacía falta que vayas allí con nosotros.

_____

9. Para poder ir a ese país necesitas vacunarte primero.

_____

10. El profesor me dijo que yo no debía sentarme junto a Jorge.

_____

Exercise 3

Fill in the blanks with an appropriate tense or construction of the verbs in parentheses.

1. ¡Otra vez te duele la barriga! ¡No _____ (deber comer) tanto chocolate!

2. _____ (Poder ser) que Marta tuviera que repetir el último examen.

3. Las luces de la casa están encendidas, así que Antonio ya

   _____ (deber de llegar).

4. Las tiendas ya han cerrado. Nosotros _____

   (deber salir) bastante antes.

5. Mucho me temo que esta lavadora ya no _____

   (funcionar).

6. Ayer no fui a la oficina, porque no _____ (tener

   que trabajar). No me tocaba.

7. No _____ (hacer falta) que nadie me lo dijera. Lo

   averigüé yo solo.

8. Tú no _____ (deber estar) con ese hombre ayer.

   _____ (Poder ser) peligroso.

9. Ella comentó que nosotros _____ (deber de tener)

   mucho dinero, a juzgar por la casa en la que vivíamos.

10. Creo que tú _____ (poder estudiar) mucho más

    para el examen de ayer.

Conditional Sentences

Conditional sentences imply a certain action if another action takes place first. Once again, Spanish and English both show notable similarities in usage.

Types and Variations

Conditional sentences have two parts: the main clause and the **si** (*if*) clause. There are three kinds of conditional sentences and certain variations within each kind.

Type 1: Probable

If the verb in the **si** clause is in the present tense of the indicative mood, the verb in the main clause is in the future. It doesn't matter which comes first:

Si llueve, no iremos a la playa.	If it rains, we won't go to the beach.
Aprobarás si estudias un poco.	You will pass if you study a little.
Si Juan viene, cenaremos en el jardín.	If Juan comes, we will have dinner in the garden.

Inversion of the subject is very common in the **si** clause:

Si viene Luis, no iremos a la fiesta.	If Luis comes, we won't go to the party.

Type 2: Possible

If the verb in the *si* clause is in the past tense of the subjunctive, the verb in the main clause is in the conditional:

Si tuviera dinero, compraría ese coche.	If I had money, I would buy that car.
Yo no haría eso si yo fuera tú.	I wouldn't do that if I were you.
Ella aprobaría si estudiara más.	She would pass if she studied harder.

Inversion of the subject in the *si* clause is also very common:

Si estuviera tu padre aquí...	If your father were here . . .

Type 3: Past Condition

If the verb in the *si* clause is in the ***pretérito pluscuamperfecto*** of the subjunctive, the verb in the main clause is in the conditional perfect:

Si hubieras estado allí, habrías visto a la reina de Inglaterra.	If you had been there, you would have seen the Queen of England.
Ellos habrían vendido su casa si hubieran necesitado el dinero.	They would have sold their house if they had needed the money.

Many Spanish speakers use the ***pluscuamperfecto*** of the subjunctive in the main clause instead of the conditional perfect:

Ella hubiera aprobado si hubiera estudiado más.	She would have passed if she had studied harder.

As in the preceding examples, inversion of the subject is also possible:

Si hubiera venido Ana,...	If Ana had come, . . .

Variations

As you can see, Spanish and English share similarities in how they express the conditional. Even the variations that appear in English have a similar construction in Spanish:

Si hay niebla, puede que los aviones no despeguen.	If it is foggy, the planes may/ might not take off.
Si estás cansado, puedes irte.	If you are tired you can/may go.
Si para de llover, podemos ir a la playa.	If it stops raining we can go to the beach.
Si quieres aprobar, debes/deberías estudiar más.	If you want to pass, you must/ should study harder.
Si quieres ese empleo, escríbele pronto.	If you want that job, write to him soon.
Si ves a Felipe, ¿podrías decirle que no voy a venir esta noche?	If you see Felipe, could you tell him that I'm not going to come tonight?
Si calientas el hielo, se convierte en agua.	If you heat ice it turns into water.
Si estás estudiando, deberías apagar la radio.	If you are studying you should turn off the radio.
Si le odias, ¿por qué sales con él?	If you hate him, why do you go out with him?
Si te vas a quedar, cogeré unas mantas.	If you are going to stay, I'll pick up some blankets.
Si has terminado el examen, deberías entregarlo.	If you have finished the exam, you should hand it in.
Si lo intentaras, podrías conseguirlo.	If you tried, you could get it.

In type 2, when there is a reference to events or facts that used to happen in the past, the subjunctive mood isn't used. Instead, the ***imperfecto*** tense is used:

Si alguien abría la puerta, ella empezaba a gritar.	If somebody opened the door, she started/used to/would start screaming.
Si tú sabías que él tenía poco dinero, ¿por qué le dejaste pagar?	If you knew that he had little money, why did you let him pay?

Here are more examples with variations that are similar to English language usage:

Si él me hubiera escuchado, él sería un hombre mucho más feliz ahora.	If he had listened to me, he would be a much happier man now.
Si hubieras hecho esto, podrías haber terminado antes.	If you had done this, you could have finished before.
Si él no hubiera estado trabajando, habríamos pensado que él era culpable.	If he hadn't been working, we would have thought that he was guilty.
Si yo le hubiera enviado esta carta, ella sería mi mujer ahora.	If I had sent her this letter, she would be my wife now.

In type 3, when there is a reference to the events or facts themselves (i.e., the action did take place), the subjunctive isn't used. Instead, the **pluscuamperfecto** is used in the *si* clause, and the simple past tense is used in the main clause:

Si tú ya habías terminado, ¿por qué se enfadó ella?	If you had already finished, why did she get angry?

English sometimes uses *will* and *would* in the *if* clause. Spanish uses the present tense of the indicative of the verb **querer** for *will*, and the imperfect of the subjunctive of the same verb for *would*. This use expresses request and willingness:

Si usted quiere esperar un momento, veré si puedo encontrar la factura.	If you will wait a moment, I'll see if I can find the invoice/bill.
Si usted quisiera contarme lo que pasó, yo le podría ayudar.	If you would tell me what happened, I could help you.

There is no literal translation for *should* in *If you should see him*. Here, Spanish uses the present tense of the indicative or the **imperfecto** of the subjunctive in the *if* clause:

Si le ves, llámame.	If you see/should see him, phone me.

Si le vieras, llámame.	If you saw/should see him, phone me.

Forms Equivalent to *If*

Conditional sentences do not always have the word *if.* There are many other possibilities that usually imply the same meaning, although a few of them convey important differences. Here are all these possibilities, their uses, and their translations:

Even If/Even Though

Both forms are usually translated as **aunque**, with exactly the same use as in English. In conditional sentences, **aunque** is always followed by the subjunctive:

Debes ir con ellos aunque no te guste.	You must go with them even if you don't like it.

Whether

Whether is translated as **si**, but there are cases, especially with the verbs **gustar** and **querer,** in which it is not translated. When it is not translated, the subjunctive is required:

Irás, te guste o no.	You will go, whether you like it or not.
Tienes que decirme si estás listo o no.	You have to tell me whether you are ready or not.

Infinitives can also follow the word **si**:

No sé si comprar eso o no.	I don't know whether to buy that or not.

Unless

This linking word translates as **a no ser que** or as **a menos que**. Both forms have the same use as in English and both are followed by the subjunctive:

No aprobarás a no ser que empieces a estudiar ahora.	You won't pass unless you start to study now.

But for That

This expression can be translated by *si no*, *de no ser así*, *de lo contrario*, *de no ser por eso*, etc. None of these forms is followed by the subjunctive:

Carla me invitó. De no ser así, yo no habría venido.	Carla invited me. But for that I wouldn't have come.

Otherwise

In conditional sentences, *otherwise* can have the same translations as *but for that*:

Cogí un taxi. De lo contrario, habría llegado tarde.	I took a taxi. Otherwise I would have been late.

Provided / Providing

Both forms are translated by **con tal que/con tal de que**. The subjunctive is necessary:

Puedes coger el coche con tal (de) que no bebas.	You can take the car provided you don't drink.

Siempre que (*as long as*) can be used instead of **con tal que**:

Te lo prestaré siempre que me prometas que no vas a correr.	I will lend it to you as long as you promise me that you aren't going to speed.

Suppose / Supposing

Suppose and *supposing* translate as **supón que** if *tú* is used, and **suponga que** if **usted** is used. In the plural these forms become **suponed que** and **supongan que**. These words don't require subjunctive forms:

Supón que él tiene un accidente.	Suppose he has an accident.

What If

What if translates as **qué pasa si** in type 1, **qué pasaría si** in type 2, and **qué habría pasado si** in type 3:

¿Qué pasa si él muere?   What if he dies?
  (no subjunctive)

¿Qué pasaría si él muriera?   What if he died?
  (subjunctive)

¿Qué habría pasado si él hubiera   What if he had died?
  muerto? (subjunctive)

In Case

The correct translation for *in case* is ***por si***, and it doesn't take the subjunctive:

Limpiaré esto por si mi madre   I'll clean this in case my mother
  viene.   comes.

Inversion of the subject is frequent:

...por si lo descubre mi padre.   . . . in case my father finds out.

In case should not be translated as ***en (el) caso de que***. ***En (el) caso de que*** is a future hypothesis and is mainly used in sentences in which the speaker is talking about measures to be taken if something happens. In such cases the subjunctive is required:

En el caso de que se averíe, usted   If it breaks down, you will be
  podrá usar la garantía.   able to use the guarantee.

In warnings, *in case of* translates as ***en caso de***:

En caso de incendio romper el   In case of fire break the glass.
  cristal.

There is a tendency to use infinitive forms in imperatives in public signs, which include warnings. The one who writes the warning doesn't know in advance who this warning is going to be read by. ***Romped el cristal*** implies the use of ***vosotros***; ***Rompan el cristal*** implies the use of ***ustedes***. To avoid this, the infinitive is used (***Romper el cristal***).

If Only / I Wish

Both forms translate as **Ojalá**, which always requires the subjunctive. **Ojalá** is never preceded by subjects:

Ojalá ella venga a tiempo.	If only she comes in time.
Ojalá él nos ayude.	If only he will help us.
Ojalá no vivieras aquí.	If only you didn't live here.
Ojalá no hubieras comprado eso.	If only you hadn't bought that.
Ojalá parara de llover.	I wish it would stop raining.

Will and *would* are not translated in sentences with **ojalá**. Present and past tense of the subjunctive are used instead.

Exercise 1

Correct any mistakes.

1. Si no entregas ese ejercicio, no podré aprobarte.

_____

2. Tu padre no te prestaría el auto a no ser que le prometas que no vas a correr.

_____

3. Siempre que me necesitas estaré a tu entera disposición.

_____

4. Ojalá yo sea más alto; así podría jugar al baloncesto.

_____

5. Tendremos que ir al hospital si el médico no venga pronto.

_____

6. Yo no les llevaría al cine si hubiera sabido que la película era así.

_____

7. Si María me dijera sí, yo sería el hombre más feliz del mundo.

_____

8. Si hicieras un poco de deporte, adelgazarás más rápido.

_____

9. Nada malo ocurrirá con tal que haces lo que yo digo.

_____

10. Si me hubieses avisado, habría ido a recogerte a la estación.

_____

Exercise 2

Fill in the blanks with an appropriate tense of the verbs in parentheses. The tenses and moods of the verbs should correspond to those described in this chapter as type 1, 2, 3, and possible variations. Omit subject pronouns as much as possible.

1. Si _____ (tú desayunar) bien esta mañana, ahora

   no _____ (tú tener) tanta hambre.

2. Ojalá _____ (llegar) pronto Fernando. De lo

   contrario _____ (nosotros perder) el tren de las

   once.

3. ¿Qué _____ (pasar) si _____

   (nosotros perder) la carrera de mañana?

4. Si me _____ (tú hacer) caso el otro día, no

   _____ (tú tener) tantos problemas.

5. Elena _____ (conocer) a los padres de Jorge si

   _____ (ella ir) a su fiesta de cumpleaños la

   semana pasada.

6. Si _____ (hacer) mal tiempo esta tarde,

   _____ (quedarnos) en casa.

7. Si _____ (yo ser) político, nunca

   _____ (yo mentir).

8. ¿Qué _____ (tú ir) a hacer si

   _____ (venir) Juan esta noche?

9. No sé si _____ (vender) la casa o

   _____ (esperar) a que el mercado se reponga.

10. Ojalá _____ (tú estar) allí con nosotros el año

    pasado.

Exercise 3

Join the following sentences as in the examples.

Juan no compró el periódico. No se enteró de lo sucedido.
Si Juan hubiera comprado el periódico, se habría enterado de lo sucedido.
Quizás mañana llueva. Si es así, no iremos a la playa.
Si mañana llueve, no iremos a la playa./Si mañana lloviera, no iríamos a la playa.

1. Es posible que Enrique traiga el auto. Si es así, podremos ir todos juntos.

   _____

2. Federico no estuvo en Londres ese año. Él no conoció a Marta.

   _____

3. Antonio no pudo reparar la tubería. Él no tenía los utensilios adecuados.

   _____

4. Mis padres no me quisieron dar permiso para ir a la fiesta. Sabían que iba a haber alcohol.

   _____

5. No comprendí nada de la película. Estaba en versión original.

   _____

6. Es probable que Tomás acepte ese empleo. Si es así, se mudará a Los Ángeles.

   _____

7. Javier no pudo encontrar la dirección. No tenía un plano.

_____

8. Los clientes se marcharon. No quedaba cerveza.

_____

9. No estuve en Inglaterra. No pude aprender inglés.

_____

10. Esos pueblos se inundaron. Los diques se rompieron.

_____

Quick-Glance Tables

Ser vs. *Estar*

Remember that **ser** is used with fixed qualities, and **estar** refers to temporary qualities and situations. Apart from this general rule, both verbs have their specific uses. This table will help you make the right choice.

	Ser	*Estar*
Designation of people, animals and things	✓	
Usual profession/occupation	✓	
Temporary profession/occupation	✓	
What somebody/something becomes	✓	
Property	✓	
Characteristics that are always true	✓	
Indication of place/time of event	✓	
Passive constructions	✓	
Introducing reasons and excuses	✓	
Situation and position		✓
Temporary characteristics		✓
Progressive/continuous tenses		✓
Semipassive structures		✓
Changes in characteristics		✓
Marital, economic, and social status	✓	✓
Reference to moment of speaking		✓
English adjectives ending in *-ed*		✓
English adjectives ending in *-ing*	✓	

Infinitive or Gerund

In order to avoid mistakes caused by literal translations (*I like fishing* should be **Me gusta pescar**, not **Me gusta pescando**), this table shows when gerunds and infinitives should be used in Spanish.

	Infinitive	*Gerund*
Subject of the sentence	✓	
After prepositions	✓	
After verbs, expressing *how* something is done		✓
After verbs, expressing *what* is being done		✓
Giving directions		✓
After verbs, expressing joy, suffering, etc.		✓
Expressing *when* something *happened*		✓
Expressing *when* something *will* happen		✓
Expressing condition		✓
Expressing reason	✓	
After verbs, except in preceding cases	✓	

To Be or *to Have*

There are many cases in which Spanish uses *to have* when English uses *to be*. This table will help you make the right choice.

	Ser	*Estar*	*Tener*
Questions with *qué* + noun:			
Age (***edad***)			✓
Height (***altura/estatura***)			✓
Length (***longitud***)			✓
Width (***anchura***)			✓
Depth (***profundidad***)			✓
Size (***tamaño/talla***)			✓
Weight (***peso***)			✓
Answer to these questions			✓

	Ser	Estar	Tener
Questions with *cuál*:			
Age	✓		
Height	✓		
Length	✓		
Width	✓		
Depth	✓		
Size	✓		
Weight	✓		
Answer to these questions	✓		
With certain English adjectives:			
Wrong (*equivocado*)		✓	
Right (*razón*)			✓

Simple Present and Present Continuous

Remember that the present continuous is formed with the verb *estar* and the gerund. It is almost exclusively used to refer to actions that are taking place *at* or *around* the moment of speaking. The simple present is used more in Spanish.

Cases	*Simple*	*Continuous*
Habits	✓	
Facts	✓	
Rules and laws	✓	
With adverbs of frequency	✓	
Intentions (future)	✓	
Plans (future)	✓	
Arrangement	✓	
Promises	✓	
Threats	✓	
Predictions	✓	
Conditionals, type 1 (*if* part)	✓	

Cases	Simple	Continuous
Offers and suggestions (*shall I/we*)	✓	
Actions *at* the moment of speaking	✓	✓
Actions *around* the moment of speaking	(✓)	✓
Changes and development	(✓)	✓
Corrections to express changes	(✓)	✓
Corrections to avoid misunderstandings	(✓)	✓

(The parentheses indicate that it is less advisable.)

Imperfecto and *Pretérito indefinido*

Remember that the **imperfecto** is used to refer to actions or situations that were still happening or were still true *at* or *around* the past moment referred to. The **pretérito indefinido** refers to actions that were completed in the past.

Cases	Imperfecto	Pretérito Indefinido
Habits	✓	
Facts	✓	
With adverbs of frequency	✓	
Intentions (future of the past)	✓	
Plans (future of the past)	✓	
Arrangements (future of the past)	✓	
Promises in the future of the past	✓	
Threats in the future of the past	✓	
Predictions (future of the past)	✓	
Conditionals, type 2 (*if*)	✓	
Past of shall *I/we* sentences	✓	
Actions being done *at* the moment referred to	✓	
Completed actions in the past		✓
Completed habitual situations in the past		✓
Actions known in advance	✓	
Actions not known in advance		✓

Imperfecto simple and *imperfecto continuo* (*llovía* vs. *estaba lloviendo*)

Remember that the *imperfecto continuo* is formed with the *imperfecto* of the verb *estar* and the gerund.

Cases	Imperfecto	Imperfecto Continuo
Habits	✓	
Facts	✓	
Rules and laws	✓	
With adverbs of frequency	✓	
With *siempre* (irritation, anger, etc.)		✓
Intentions (future of the past)	✓	
Plans (future of the past)	✓	
Arrangements (future of the past)	✓	
Promises	✓	
Threats	✓	
Predictions	✓	
Conditionals, reported speech (type 1)	✓	
Offers and suggestions (*shall I/we*)	✓	
Actions *at* the moment referred to	✓	✓
Actions *around* the moment referred to	(✓)	✓
Changes and development	(✓)	✓
Corrections to express changes	(✓)	✓
Corrections to avoid misunderstandings	(✓)	✓

(The parentheses indicate that it is less advisable.)

Pretérito indefinido and *pretérito perfecto* (*llovió* vs. *ha llovido*)

The ***pretérito perfecto*** is formed with the present of the verb ***haber*** and a past participle. It is used to refer to completed actions in the recent past. Spanish speakers in Latin America prefer the ***pretérito indefinido***. This table is based on uses in Spain.

Cases	Pretérito Indefinido	Pretérito Perfecto
Actions completed in the recent past (today, this week, this month, etc.)		✓
Actions completed in a more remote past	✓	
With words that indicate the past (*ayer*, *la semana pasada*, etc.)	✓	
Completed actions in the present		✓
Actions that embrace a long period (up to now)		✓
Questions about something recent		✓
Questions about an action in the past	✓	
Questions from a remote past up to now		✓
Noticing something for the first time		✓
Reaction to something noticed for the first time		✓

Present, Future, and *ir + a*

This table shows the different tenses that can be used in talking about the future. Remember that the construction *ir a* never uses gerunds when intentions or plans are meant.

Cases	Present	Future	Ir a (Present)
Decision taken at the moment of speaking	✓	(✓)	
Plans	✓		✓
Intentions	✓		✓
Arrangements	✓		✓
Promises	✓	✓	✓
Threats	✓	✓	✓

Cases	Present	Future	Ir a (Present)
General predictions		✓	✓
Predictions with high degree of certainty	✓	✓	✓
Requests (verb **querer**)	✓		
Future action that is part of a routine	✓	✓	✓
Future actions that express a strong decision	✓	✓	✓
Future actions with doubts	✓	✓	✓
Supposing about the present	✓	✓	
Supposing about the future	✓	✓	✓
Remote future		✓	

Appendix

Verbs and Prepositions

This appendix offers a selection of common verbs and the prepositions that usually go with them. The example sentences provided with each entry demonstrate how to incorporate the verb/preposition combinations into well-constructed sentences.

A

Abalanzarse **sobre** alguien:
El perro se abalanzó sobre el pobre chico.

Abogar **por** algo/alguien:
Yo abogo por la inocencia de Pablo.

Abordar **a**:
Abordé a la señora González en la tienda.

Absolver **de**:
Yo te absuelvo de todos tus pecados, hijo mío.

Abstenerse **de**:
Debes abstenerte de hacer comentarios de ese tipo.

Aburrirse **con**:
Yo me aburro mucho con las películas de miedo.

Abusar **de**:
Él siempre está abusando de los que son más débiles.

Acalorarse **con**:
Juan se acaloró con los comentarios de Jorge.

Acceder **a**:
Resulta difícil acceder a ese lugar.

Acercarse **a**:
No debes acercarte a esos animales.

Acogerse **a**:
*Quiero acogerme a esa ley para
legalizar mi situación.*

Acordarse **de**:
Siempre me acuerdo mucho de ti.

Acostumbrarse **a**:
*No puedo acostumbrarme a
conducir por la izquierda.*

Acudir **a**:
*Debes acudir a un buen médico
inmediatamente.*

Acusar **de**:
*Les acusaron de homicidio
involuntario.*

Adaptar(se) **a**:
*Esos animales no pudieron
adaptarse a vivir en un medio
tan hostil.*

Adelantarse **a** alguien, **en** algo:
*Los japoneses se adelantaron a los
europeos en el terreno de la
electrónica.*

Admirarse **de**:
*Me admiro de la inteligencia de ese
hombre.*

Adolecer **de**:
*Adolezco de una falta crónica de
vitamina A.*

Aferrarse **a**:
*El marinero se aferró a una tabla
para no ahogarse.*

Aficionarse **a**:
*Me aficioné a beber Rioja cuando
estuve en España.*

Agarrar **a** alguien, **de/por** algo:
*Pablo agarró al ladrón del cuello
(= por el cuello).*

Alegrarse **de/con/por**:
*Me alegro mucho de tu gran éxito.
Me alegré mucho con la noticia.
Me alegro por ti.*

Alejarse **de**:
*No te alejes de la casa. Puede ser
peligroso.*

Alimentarse **con/de**:
*Dicen que Lord Byron se
alimentaba de/con raíces.*

Amenazar **a** alguien, **con** algo:
*Amenacé a mi jefe con llevarle a los
tribunales.*

Anticiparse **a**:
*Me anticipé a Pedro entregando el
proyecto primero.*

Añadir **a**:
*Quiero añadir unas cuantas cosas
a tus comentarios.*

Apasionarse **por**:
*Me apasioné por la música clásica
cuando estuve en Austria.*

Apelar **a**:
*Tendremos que apelar al Tribunal
Constitucional.*

Apiadarse **de**:
Apiádate de nosotros, Señor.

Aplicar(se) **a**:
*Aplicaré todos mis conocimientos al
descubrimiento de esa vacuna.*

Apoderarse **de**:
*Me apoderé de los documentos sin
que se dieran cuenta.*

Aprender **a** + infinitivo:
Necesito aprender a nadar pronto.

Apropiarse **de**:
*Te has apropiado de todas mis
cosas.*

Aprovecharse **de**:
*No te debes aprovechar de la
inocencia de esa chica.*

Aproximarse **a**:
*Nos estamos aproximando a Nueva
York.*

Arremeter **contra**:
*Arremetí contra él con todas mis
fuerzas y le derribé.*

Arrepentirse **de**:
*Algún día te arrepentirás de lo que
me has hecho.*

Arriesgarse **a**:
*No debes arriesgarte a que te
pillen.*

Arrimarse **a**:
*No quiero que te arrimes al borde
del precipicio.*

Arrinconar **a** alguien **en** un lugar:
*La policía arrinconó a ese ladrón
en un callejón.*

Arrojar **a** alguien **de/por** la
ventana/puerta, etc.:
*La fuerza de la explosión arrojó a
la mujer por la ventana.*

Arropar(se) **con**:
*Me arropé con una vieja manta
que encontré allí.*

Asociarse **a/con**:
*No quiero asociarme con gente que
está bajo sospecha.*

Asomarse **a**:
*Ella no quiso asomarse a la
ventana para verme.*

Asombrarse **con**:
Me asombré con lo que hiciste.

Aspirar **a**:
Aspiro a ser millonario algún día.

Asustarse **de/con/por**:
¿Por qué te asustas de mí?
Me asusté con los datos que me
*   dieron.*
Ella se asustó por la presencia de
*   aquel hombre.*

Atemorizarse **de/por**:
Te atemorizaste de ver que venía
*   la policía.*
Ella se atemorizó por las
*   amenazas.*

Atender **a**:
Tengo que atender a mis invitados.

Atenerse **a**:
Tendrás que atenerte a las
*   consecuencias.*

Atentar **contra**:
El terrorista quiso atentar contra el
*   presidente.*

Atragantarse **con**:
Me atraganté con un hueso de
*   aceituna.*

Atribuir **a**:
No puedes atribuir tus fracasos a
*   los demás.*

Ausentarse **de**:
Pablo va a ausentarse de su
*   domicilio durante dos semanas.*

Avanzar **a/hacia/hasta**:
El barco avanzaba hacia la costa.
Avancé hasta la esquina.

Avenirse **a**:
Ella no quiere avenirse a nuestras
*   razones.*

Avergonzarse **de/por**:
Juan se avergonzaba de su padre.

Ayudar **a**:
Debemos ayudar a esos pobres
*   niños.*

B

Batallar **con**:
Siempre estoy batallando con mis
*   alumnos.*

Beber **de** un vaso, la botella, etc.:
Debes beber de un vaso, no de la
*   botella de la que bebemos todos.*

Besar **en** la cara:
La besé en la cara, no en la boca.

Bregar **con**:
Estoy agotado. He estado bregando
*   con mis niños todo el día.*

Brotar **de/en**:
El manantial brota de/en una
*   cueva.*

Burlarse **de**:
No debes burlarte de tus profesores.

C

Calificar **a** alguien **de** algo:
Ella calificó a su marido de
violento.

Cansarse **con/de**:
Me cansé de tanto hablar.
Yo me canso mucho con los niños.

Carecer **de**:
Carecemos de cosas elementales
para montar el negocio.

Cargar **de**:
Los obreros cargaron el camión de
madera.

Casarse **con**:
¿Por qué no te casaste con ella?

Ceder **a**:
No voy a ceder a tus pretensiones.

Ceñirse **a**:
Debes ceñirte a lo que dice el
guión.

Cerciorarse **de**:
Cerciórate de que no hay nadie ahí
fuera.

Cesar **de**:
A las seis cesó de llover.

Circunscribirse **a**:
Debemos circunscribirnos a las
normas establecidas por el
comité.

Cojear **de**:
Jorge cojea del pie derecho.

Combatir **con/contra** las tropas:
Yo también combatí contra las
tropas de los militares golpistas.

Comerciar **en** artículos:
El señor Valdés comercia en
antigüedades.

Compadecerse **de**:
Me compadecí de ellos y les dejé
libres.

Compartir algo **con** alguien:
No quiero compartir mi habitación
con él.

Compensar algo **con** algo:
Tendremos que compensar el
tiempo perdido con horas extra.

Competir **con**:
Nuestra economía no puede
competir con los precios de ese
país.

Componerse **de**:
Una molécula de agua se compone
de dos átomos de hidrógeno y
uno de oxígeno.

Comprometerse **a** algo, **con**
alguien:
Me comprometí con Elena a
ayudarla con sus deberes.

Concurrir **a**:
Ese partido político no puede
concurrir a las próximas
elecciones.

Condenar **a** alguien **a** algo:
El juez condenó a Pedro a tres
meses de cárcel.

Condolerse **de**:
No debes condolerte de algo que no
es tu culpa.

Confiar **en**:
Tendremos que confiar en ellos.

Confirmarse **en**:
Ellos se confirmaron en sus ideas.

Conformarse **con**:
Tendrás que conformarte con lo
que ya tienes.

Confundir **con**:
La confundí con otra persona.

Congeniar **con**:
No pude congeniar con mi suegra.

Congraciarse **con**:
Me congracié con los niños
dándoles caramelos.

Congratularse **de/por**:
Me congratulo de tu buena suerte.

Consistir **en**:
Todo el problema consiste en hablar
con el director.

Consolarse **con**:
Tuve que consolarme con el tercer
premio.

Constar **de** algo, **en** un
documento:
La casa consta de tres habitaciones.
Mi nombre no consta en ese
documento.

Contagiarse **con/de**:
Me contagié de la enfermedad que
tenían ellos.

Contaminarse **con/de**:
Las aguas se contaminaron con los
vertidos.

Contar **con** algo o alguien:
Cuento contigo para organizarlo
todo.

Contentarse **con**:
Me tendré que contentar con ese
sueldo.

Contestar **a** una pregunta:
El alumno no supo contestar a mi
pregunta.

Contribuir **a** algo **con** dinero:
Voy a contribuir a esa causa con
dos mil dólares.

Convalecer **de**:
Ahora convalecen del accidente que tuvieron hace un mes.

Convencerse **de** algo:
Me convencí de que ellos me estaban engañando.

Conversar **con** alguien **sobre** algo:
Estuve conversando con el profesor sobre los problemas de la comunidad.

Convertir algo **en** algo:
La bruja convirtió al príncipe en rana.

Convertirse **en**:
En sólo cinco años, Juan se convirtió en el presidente de la compañía.

Corresponderse **con**:
Estos datos no se corresponden con la realidad.

Cubrirse **con/de**:
Me cubrí con una chaqueta.
El cuerpo estaba cubierto de hojas.

Culpar **a** alguien **de** algo:
Culparon a Jacinto de todos los robos que se habían cometido.

Cumplir **con**:
Tengo que cumplir con un horario muy estricto.

Curarse **de**:
Ella intenta curarse de su enfermedad en una clínica en las montañas.

D

Darse **a** una actividad, **contra** algo:
Él se dio a la bebida cuando su mujer le dejó.
Me di un golpe contra un árbol.

Decidirse **a** + infinitivo:
Me decidí a participar en esa carrera.

Decidirse **por** algo:
Al final me decidí por el coche rojo.

Dedicar algo **a** algo:
Él dedica todo su dinero a hacer el bien.

Dedicarse **a**:
Me dedico a traducir libros.

Dejarse **de**:
Déjate de tonterías.

Depender **de**:
Yo todavía dependo de mis padres.

Desayunar(se) **con**:
No suelo desayunar con té.

Descansar **de** una actividad:
Necesito descansar de mi trabajo de vez en cuando.

Descollar **en** una cualidad:
No te preocupes. No puedes descollar en todas las asignaturas.

Desconfiar **de**:
Desconfío de ese hombre.

Descontar **de** una cantidad:
Descontaré el tiempo perdido de tu próximo salario.

Descuidarse **de/en**:
No debes descuidarte de tus obligaciones.

Desdecirse **de**:
Ella se desdijo de lo que había asegurado el día antes.

Desembarazarse **de**:
Deberías desembarazarte de todas estas viejas cosas.

Desembocar **en**:
Ese río desemboca en el Atlántico.

Desengañarse **de**:
Me desengañé de la mala voluntad de mis compañeros.

Desenterrar **de**:
Lo desenterraron de su tumba.

Desfallecer **de**:
Ellos desfallecían de hambre.

Deshacerse **de** algo:
Te deberías deshacer de todo eso.

Desistir **de**:
Tuve que desistir de mis pretensiones.

Despedirse **de**:
Me despedí de mis amigos en el aeropuerto.

Despoblarse **de**:
Estos pueblos se han despoblado de jóvenes en los últimos diez años.

Desprenderse **de**:
Mi abuela no quiere desprenderse de esas viejas fotos.

Destinar algo **a** algo:
Voy a destinar cinco mil dólares a la lucha contra el cáncer.

Destinar **a** alguien **a** algún lugar:
Destinaron a Javier a Londres como encargado de negocios en la embajada.

Desviarse **de**:
No te desvíes de este sendero. Te podrías perder.

Detenerse **a** + infinitivo:
Elena se detuvo a descansar durante unos minutos.

Discrepar **de** una opinión:
Discrepo de lo que acabas de decir sobre los inmigrantes.

Disculparse **con** alguien **de/por** algo:
Me disculpé con Pedro por haber abollado su coche.

Disfrazarse **de** médico **con** una bata:
Patricia se disfrazó de fantasma con una vieja sábana.

Disfrutar **de**:
Estamos disfrutando de unas merecidas vacaciones.

Disgustarse **con** alguien **por** algo:
Me disgusté con mi hija por su mal comportamiento.

Disponerse **a** + infinitivo:
Juan se disponía a salir cuando el teléfono empezó a sonar.

Distinguirse **de** otros **por** algo:
Ella se distingue de los demás por su afán de superación.

Distraerse **con**:
Ese niño se distrae con una mosca volando.

Distribuir algo **entre** personas:
Tenemos que distribuir todos estos paquetes entre nuestros clientes.

Disuadir **a** alguien **de** hacer algo:
La policía disuadió a los manifestantes de continuar hasta el ayuntamiento.

Divertirse **con**:
Yo me divierto mucho con mis niños.

Dividir **en** partes, **por** la mitad, **entre** gente:
Dividí el pastel en cuatro partes iguales.
Ella dividió su fortuna por la mitad entre sus dos hijos.

Divorciarse **de**:
Paulino se divorció de su mujer.

Dolerse **de**:
Ella se duele mucho de la espalda.

Dotar **a** alguien **de/con** algo:
Voy a dotar a mi hijo con una asignación mensual de 1000 dólares.

Dudar **de**:
Veo que dudas de mí.

E

Echar **a** alguien **de** un lugar:
Eché a Antonio de mi oficina.

Ejercitarse **en/con** algo:
Me estoy ejercitando en el submarinismo.
Ella siempre se ejercita con pesas.

Elevarse **a/hasta** un lugar:
El cohete se elevó hasta las nubes.

Embadurnar algo, **a** alguien **de** algo:
La pequeña embadurnó el sofá de miel.
Yo embadurné a Ana de alquitrán.

Embarcarse **en** un barco **para** Londres:
Me embarqué en un submarino.
Me embarcaré para Rotterdam la semana que viene.

Embelesarse **con**:
Ella siempre se embelesa con los dibujos animados.

Embestir **contra**:
El toro embistió contra el caballo.

Embobarse **con**:
Agustín siempre se emboba con todo lo que le dice su novia.

Emborracharse **de**:
Emborracharse de champán no es lo mismo que emborracharse de vino.

Embravecerse **con/contra**:
La multitud se embraveció contra los policías.

Empacharse **de**:
Te vas a empachar de pastel.

Empalagarse **de**:
Terminarás empalagándote de caramelos.

Empalmar algo **con** algo:
He empalmado estas dos piezas con un trozo de goma.

Emparentar **con**:
Si te casas con ella, emparentarás con la reina.

Empeñarse **en** algo:
Me empeñé en conseguir ese empleo.

Emplearse **en** algo:
Ella se está empleando a fondo en la preparación del campeonato.

Empotrarse **en/contra**:
El coche se empotró contra un pilar del puente.

Enajenarse **de**:
*No debemos enajenarnos de esas
propiedades.*

Enamorarse **de**:
Me enamoré de una bailarina.

Encajar algo **con/en** algo:
*Tu teoría no encaja con/en lo que
sucedió realmente.*

Encaminarse **a/hacia**:
*Las tropas se encaminan hacia la
frontera.*

Encapricharse **con**:
*Me he encaprichado con un coche
deportivo.*

Encaramarse **a** un lugar, **en** un
árbol:
El ladrón se encaramó al balcón.
*Los niños se encaramaron a ese
árbol.*

Encararse **a/con** alguien:
*Me encaré con Miguel por lo que le
dijo a mi mujer.*

Encargarse **de**:
*Quiero que te encargues de
organizarlo todo.*

Encogerse **de** hombros:
*Cuando se lo conté, Paco se encogió
de hombros y se marchó.*

Encomendarse **a**:
*Me he encomendado a todos los
santos para que todo salga bien
en la operación.*

Enconarse **con**:
*Los chinos se enconaron con los
japoneses por cuestiones
comerciales.*

Encontrarse **con** alguien:
*Ayer me encontré con Pedro por la
calle.*

Endurecerse **con/en/por**:
Esto se endurece con el agua.
Ella se endureció en los tribunales.
*Me endurecí por los avatares de la
vida.*

Enemistarse **con**:
*Nos hemos enemistado con nuestros
vecinos.*

Enfadarse **con** alguien, **por** algo:
*Me enfadé con ella por lo que le
hizo a Jaime.*

Enfermar **de**:
Ana enfermó de viruela.

Enfrascarse **en**:
*Me enfrasqué en una discusión
estúpida.*

Enfurecerse **con** alguien, **por** algo:
Ella se enfureció con su jefe por el comentario que él había hecho.

Engalanarse **con**:
Ese día, las chicas se engalanan con trajes regionales.

Engolfarse **con/en**:
Te estás engolfando en los juegos de cartas.

Engreírse **con**:
Te vas a engreír con tanto dinero.

Enlazar algo **con** algo:
Hemos enlazado nuestro viaje de negocios con nuestras vacaciones.

Enloquecer **de**:
Juan enloqueció de amor.

Enojarse **con** alguien, **de/por** algo:
Me enojé con Agustín por sus malas notas.

Enredarse algo **con/en** algo:
La hélice se enredó en las algas.

Enriquecerse **con**:
Ellos se enriquecieron con el contrabando.

Enseñar **a** + infinitivo:
Te voy a enseñar a calcular eso sin calculadora.

Entender **de** algo:
Él entiende mucho de coches.

Entenderse **con** alguien:
Mi hijo se entiende muy bien con sus profesores.

Enterarse **de**:
Me he enterado de que te vas a casar.

Entremeterse **en**:
No quiero que te entremetas en esa polémica.

Entretenerse **con** algo:
Ese niño se entretiene con cualquier cosa.

Entristecerse **con/de/por**:
Me entristecí mucho por la muerte de mi profesor.

Envanecerse **con/de/en**:
Ella se envaneció con sus muchos triunfos.

Envejecer **con/de/por** algo, **en** un lugar:
Me gustaría envejecer con mi mujer.
Ella envejeció de sufrimiento.
Envejecí por el hambre.
Quiero envejecer en mi pueblo.

Enviciarse **en/con**:
José se está enviciando con las máquinas tragaperras.

Envolverse **con/en/entre**:
Ella se envolvió en una sábana.

Enzarzarse **en**:
Me enzarcé en una pelea.

Equipar **a** alguien **con/de** algo:
Tenemos que equipar a nuestros chicos con mejores indumentarias.

Equiparar algo/**a** alguien **a/con**:
Equiparé a Antonio con Luis.

Equivocarse **en** algo, **con** alguien:
Me equivoqué en el último ejercicio.
Te has equivocado conmigo.

Escabullirse **entre/por entre**:
El conejo se escabulló (por) entre los arbustos.

Escarmentar **con**:
Vas a escarmentar con este castigo ejemplar.

Escoger **entre** posibilidades:
Ella tuvo que escoger entre el inglés y el alemán.

Esconderse **de** alguien, **en** algún lugar:
¿Por qué te escondes de la policía?
Nos escondimos en una cochera.

Esforzarse **por**:
Debes esforzarte por unas mejores notas.

Esmerarse **en**:
Esmérate en esa tarea.

Estrellarse **contra**:
Me estrellé contra un árbol.

Estrenarse **con**:
Como actor, Jorge se estrenó con una obra de teatro.

Examinarse **de**:
Mañana me examino del carnet de conducir.

Excederse **de**:
Creo que ella se excede de limpia.

Excluir algo/**a** alguien **de** algo:
Voy a excluir a Tomás de esas ventajas.

Exponerse **a**:
No debes exponerte a peligros innecesarios.

Extenderse **hasta**:
El imperio Árabe se extendía hasta la Península Ibérica.

Extrañarse **de**:
¿De qué te extrañas?
Me extraño de que tengas tanto dinero de repente.

F

Fastidiarse **con**:
*Me fastidié con la visita de mis
    vecinos.*

Fatigarse **de**:
Ella se fatigó de trabajar.

Favorecerse **de**:
*No te puedes favorecer de las
    desgracias de los demás.*

Fiarse **de**:
No me fío de ti.

Fijarse **en**:
Fíjate en esa chica.

Fluctuar **entre**:
*El precio fluctúa entre los dos y los
    tres dólares.*

Forrar algo **de/con/en**:
Me voy a forrar de dinero.

Franquearse **con**:
*Necesito franquearme con mi
    mujer.*

Freír **con/en**:
*Es mejor freír esto en aceite de
    oliva.*

Fumar **en** pipa:
Mi abuelo siempre fumaba en pipa.

G

Ganar **a** algún deporte:
Gané algún dinero a las cartas.

Gastar dinero **en**:
¿Cuánto gastas en electricidad?

Girar **a/hacia**:
*Ahora debes girar a/hacia la
    derecha.*

Gozar **con**:
Yo gozo con el baile.

Gravar algo **con**:
*Estas fincas van a ser gravadas con
    un impuesto especial.*

Guardarse **de**:
Guárdate de los amigos lisonjeros.

Guarecerse **de** la tormenta, **en** un
    lugar:
*Me guarecí de la lluvia en una
    parada de autobús.*

Guiarse **por**:
*Los marineros se guían por las
    estrellas.*

H

Habérselas **con**:
*Tendrás que habértelas conmigo si
    haces eso otra vez.*

Habituarse **a**:
No puedo habituarme a vivir sin ella.

Hablar **con** alguien, **de/sobre** algo:
Hablé con ellos sobre la nueva situación.

Hacerse **a** algo nuevo, **con/de** cosas:
Tendrás que hacerte a tu nueva situación.
Juan se ha hecho de mucho dinero en los últimos años.

Hartarse **de**:
Me harté de comer.

Helarse **de**:
Te vas a helar de frío.

Henchir algo **de** algo:
Están henchidos de orgullo y vanidad.

Heredar **de** alguien:
Heredé dos casas de mi abuelo.

Hermanarse **con**:
Veinte años después de la guerra, Francia se hermanó con Alemania.

Hincarse **de**:
Me hinqué de rodillas.

Honrarse **con** algo, **de** + infinitivo:
Me honro con tu presencia.
Me honro de ser el mejor arquitecto de la ciudad.

Huir **a/de** un lugar:
Los ladrones huyeron a otra ciudad.
Los ladrones huyeron de la cárcel.

I

Igualar algo/**a** alguien **con**, **en** + infinitivo:
No puedo igualar a Pablo con el deporte.
No puedo igualar a Pablo en hablar idiomas.

Imbuir **a** alguien **de**:
Han imbuido a tus hijos de ideas muy extrañas.

Impeler **a** alguien **a**:
Eso va a impeler a Javier a estudiar medicina.

Implicarse **con** alguien, **en** algo:
Me impliqué con ellos en un asunto muy turbio.

Importunar **a** alguien **con**:
Ella siempre está importunando a sus amigos con preguntas estúpidas.

Incitar **a** alguien **a** algo, **contra** alguien:
Incité a Sara a fumar.
Ella incitó a Miguel contra su hermano.

Incorporarse **a**:
Mañana me incorporo a mi trabajo.

Inculcar algo **en**:
Debes inculcar buenos sentimientos en tus hijos.

Incurrir **en**:
Has vuelto a incurrir en el mismo error.

Indemnizar **a** alguien **de/por**:
La compañía tiene que indemnizar a mis padres por el incendio.

Independizarse **de**:
La India se independizó de Gran Bretaña en 1947.

Indignarse **con** alguien, **por** algo:
Me indigné con Tomás por las tonterías que estaba diciendo.

Indisponer **a** alguien **contra**:
Tu versión de los hechos va a indisponer a tus hermanos contra tus padres.

Inducir **a** alguien **a** + infinitivo:
Ella fue quien indujo a Pepe a matar a su mujer.

Indultar **a** alguien **de**:
Van a indultar a Paqui de su condena.

Inferir algo **de**:
Infiero que les odias de lo que acabas de decir.

Infestar algo **con/de**:
Esto está infestado de mosquitos.

Inflamarse **de**:
El director se inflamó de ira.

Influir **en**:
Ella siempre está influyendo en su hijo.

Informar **a** alguien **de/sobre** algo:
Tengo que informar a mis superiores de lo que ha pasado.

Infundir algo **en** alguien:
¿Quién ha infundido esas ideas en tu novio?

Ingerirse **en**:
No quiero ingerirme en tu vida personal.

Inhabilitar **a** alguien **para** +
infinitivo:
Van a inhabilitar a ese hombre
para ocupar cargos públicos.

Inhibirse **de**:
Yo me inhibo de este caso.

Iniciarse **en**:
Esa mujer se inició en prácticas de
brujería.

Inquietarse **con/por**:
Me he inquietado mucho por las
noticias que diste ayer.

Insertar algo **en**:
No insertes tu nombre en ese
recuadro.

Insinuarse **a**:
Me he insinuado a tu hermana,
pero ella no quiere saber nada
de mí.

Insistir **en/sobre**:
Ellos insistieron en que yo me
quedara a cenar.

Interceder **por**:
Le he pedido a mi cuñado, que es
juez, que interceda por ti.

Interesarse **en** algo, **por** alguien:
Me intereso en esos asuntos desde
que tuve la enfermedad.
Yo me intereso mucho por ti.

Interponerse **entre**:
Nada se va a interponer entre tú y
yo.

Inundar **de**:
Han inundado mi casa de
panfletos y octavillas.

Invertir **en**:
Creo que voy a invertir en acciones
de bancos.

J

Jactarse **de**:
Ella siempre se está jactando de ser
una gran cocinera.

Jubilarse **de**:
Mi padre se jubiló de bombero a los
cincuenta años.

Jugar **a** algo:
Juego al tenis desde que tenía tu
edad.

Juntar algo **a/con** algo:
He juntado estas dos tablas con
pegamento.

Jurar **por**:
Juro por Dios que yo no lo hice.

Justificarse **de** algo:
Siempre te estás justificando de tus
errores.

L

Ladrar **a**:
*Este perro no le ladra a las
personas mayores.*

Lamentarse **de/por**:
Me lamento de no haber hecho eso.

Lanzarse **a** un lugar, **sobre** algo:
Me lancé a la piscina.
*Me lancé sobre el ladrón y le
atrapé.*

Lastimarse **con**:
*Me he lastimado con la pata de la
cama.*

Lavar **con/en**:
*No debes lavar esta ropa en agua
caliente.*

Levantarse **de**:
No podía levantarme de la cama.

Liberar **a** alguien **de** algo:
*Liberaremos a esa pobre gente de
ese tirano.*

Lidiar **con**:
*Tengo que lidiar con alumnos muy
groseros.*

Limpiar algo **de**:
*¿Cómo puedo limpiar esta camisa
de las manchas de aceite?*

Lindar **con**:
*Mis propiedades lindan con la
finca de Pedro.*

Litigar **con/contra**:
*Litigaré contra ellos hasta que me
devuelvan lo que es mío.*

Luchar **con/contra** alguien **por**
algo:
*Hemos luchado contra ellos por la
libertad.*

LL

Llamar **a**:
*Hay que llamar a una
ambulancia.*

Llegar **a** un destino, **de** un
origen:
*Llegué a Buenos Aires de Los
Ángeles el viernes.*

Llenar algo **con/de**:
Llena ese cubo de agua.

Llorar **de**:
Ella está llorando de dolor.

M

Manchar algo **con/de**:
Te has manchado de chocolate.

Maquinar **contra**:
*Estáis maquinando contra mí para
conseguir mi puesto de trabajo.*

Maravillarse **con/de**:
Yo siempre me maravillo con las cosas que dices.

Mediar **entre** personas, **por** alguien:
Hay que mediar entre ellos para que vuelvan a estar juntos.
Hay que mediar por Joaquín para que le readmitan en la fábrica.

Meditar **sobre**:
Estoy meditando sobre lo que me dijiste ayer.

Medrar **en**:
No puedes medrar en la política.

Mesurarse **en**:
Debes mesurarte en tus opiniones. Eres demasiado radical.

Mofarse **de**:
Se mofaron de mí.

Molestar **a** alguien **con**:
No quiero molestar a tus padres con mis problemas.

Montar **en** vehículos, **a** caballo:
¿Has montado en barco alguna vez?
Nunca he montado a caballo.

Morir **de** algo:
Murieron de hambre.

Morirse **de, por** + infinitivo:
Te vas a morir de risa cuando te lo cuente.
Me muero por saber quién es el ganador.

Motejar **a** alguien **de**:
Motejaron a Pablo de imbécil.

Murmurar **de**:
Murmuran de ti todo el tiempo.

N

Necesitar algo **para**:
Necesito un martillo para clavar estos clavos.

Negarse **a**:
Me niego a participar en algo así.

Nombrar **a** alguien **para**:
Han nombrado a mi hermano para ese puesto.

Nutrirse **con/de**:
Estos animales se nutren generalmente de carroña.

O

Obedecer **a**:
Yo sólo obedezco a mis padres.
Esto obedece a un error cometido en el sistema central.

Obligar **a** alguien **a**:
Hay que obligar a los alumnos a
que hagan esto.

Obstinarse **en**:
Veo que te obstinas en pensar que
yo lo hice.

Obtener algo **de**:
Obtuve grandes beneficios de esas
inversiones.

Ocultar algo **a/de**:
No debes ocultarle la verdad a tus
amigos.
No debes ocultar esto de la gente
que te quiere.

Ocuparse **de**:
Yo no me ocupo de los transportes
internos.

Ofenderse **por**:
Ella se ofendió por mi comentario.

Ofrecerse **a** alguien, **de/como**
  algo:
Me ofrecí a mi vecina como
profesor de su hijo.

Oler **a**:
Esto huele a gasolina.

Olvidarse **de**:
No te olvides de mí.

Opinar **de/sobre**:
Tengo que opinar sobre tu conducta
de ayer.

Oponerse **a**:
Me opongo a estas medidas tan
injustas.

Optar **por**:
Opté por invitar a su hermana.

Orar **a** Dios **por** alguien:
Oremos a Dios por el alma de estos
pobres desgraciados.

P

Pactar algo **con** alguien:
Hemos pactado nuevas condiciones
con el sindicato.

Padecer **de** una enfermedad:
Esa pobre mujer padece de artrosis.

Pararse **a** + infinitivo:
Párate a pensar en lo que has
hecho.

Parecerse **a**:
Yo me parezco más a mi padre.

Partir **a/para** un destino, **de** un
  origen:
Mañana partimos para Londres.
El barco partió del puerto de
Londres.

Pasar **de** algo **a** algo:
Vamos a pasar de este asunto a otro
mucho más importante.

Pelear **por** algo:
Debes pelear por tus convicciones.

Pelearse **con** alguien **por** algo:
Me peleé con mi mejor amigo por
una chica.

Pensar **en/sobre**:
Estoy siempre pensando en ti.

Perecer **de**:
Perecieron de hambre.

Perfumar **con**:
Quiero perfumar esta habitación
con fragancias orientales.

Permanecer **en**:
Tengo que permanecer en el
hospital hasta el lunes.

Permutar algo **con/por**:
Hemos permutado esta máquina
por una furgoneta.

Perseverar **en**:
Hay que perseverar en nuestras
posiciones políticas.

Persistir **en**:
Los jefes persisten en querer
despedir personal.

Pertenecer **a**:
Esa casa perteneció a mis abuelos
paternos.

Pertrecharse **con/de**:
Nos pertrechamos de alimentos
para pasar el invierno.

Plagarse **de**:
Después de la noticia, aquello se
plagó de periodistas.

Poblar(se) **de**:
Esta zona se pobló de ingleses.

Poder **con** algo/alguien:
No puedo con estas maletas. Son
demasiado pesadas.

Posarse **en/sobre**:
El pájaro se posó en mi mano.

Posponer algo **a**:
Tendremos que posponer la reunión
a mañana.

Precaverse **contra** algo:
Quiero precaverte contra ellos. Son
muy peligrosos.

Preceder **a** alguien:
Ella precedía a sus padres en la
ceremonia.

Preciarse **de**:
Me precio de ser el mejor amigo de
Roberto.

Prendarse **de**:
Me prendé de sus encantos.

Preocuparse **por**:
No te preocupes por mí.

Prescindir **de**:
No puedo prescindir de esos trabajadores.

Preservarse **de**:
Presérvate de las malas influencias.

Presumir **de**:
No me gusta presumir de dinero.

Prevenir **contra** algo:
Tengo que prevenirte contra las noticias que se están dando por ahí.

Pringarse **con/de**:
Me vas a pringar de chocolate como sigas comiendo así.

Privar **a** alguien **de** algo:
No puedo privar a mis hijos de la televisión.

Probar **a** + infinitivo:
Prueba a meter la llave al revés.

Promover **a** alguien **a** algo:
Han promovido a Sebastián a jefe de contabilidad.

Propagarse **a/en/por**:
La noticia se propagó por todos los clubes de la ciudad.

Propender **a**:
Ellos propenden a votar a ese partido.

Prorrumpir **en**:
Ella prorrumpió en llanto.

Proseguir **con**:
Prosigue con tu trabajo.

Protestar **contra** algo:
Vamos a protestar contra los despidos.

Proveer **a** alguien **de** algo:
Hay que proveer a esa gente de alimento cuanto antes.

Pugnar **con/contra** alguien **por** algo:
Pugnaré contra ellos por ese puesto en la empresa.

Q

Quebrarse **con/por**:
Su voz se quebró por la emoción.

Quedar **con** alguien **en** algún lugar:
He quedado con ella en el bar de la esquina.

Quedarse **a** + infinitivo:
¿Por qué no te quedas a comer?

Quejarse **a** alguien **de**:
Me quejé al director de la conducta de algunos empleados.

Querellarse **contra**:
Voy a querellarme contra ellos.

Quitar algo **de** un lugar:
Quita esto de aquí.

R

Razonar **sobre** algo:
Tienes que razonar sobre tus decisiones.

Rebajar algo **de** algo:
Rebajé veinte dólares de la factura.

Rebasar **de**:
Eso no puede rebasar de los dos mil dólares.

Rebosar **de**:
Ella rebosa de salud.

Recatarse **de**:
Deberías recatarte de comentarios así.

Recelar **de**:
Recelo de ellos.

Recobrarse **de**:
Ya me he recobrado de mi enfermedad.

Reconciliarse **con**:
Elena aún no se ha reconciliado con su marido.

Reconvenir **a** alguien **por/sobre** algo:
Tienes que reconvenir a esos alumnos por su conducta de ayer.

Recrearse **con** algo, **en** + infinitivo:
Él se recrea con acciones violentas.
No puedes recrearte en hacer daño a la gente.

Reducir algo **a**:
El fuego redujo la casa a cenizas.

Referirse **a**:
Me refiero a ese otro coche.

Reflexionar **sobre**:
Debemos reflexionar sobre las medidas que vamos a tomar.

Regodearse **con**:
Veo que te regodeas con el sufrimiento ajeno.

Reincidir **en**:
Patricia reincidió en la droga.

Reírse **de**:
No te rías de mí.

Remitirse **a**:
Me remito a los hechos.

Remontarse **a**:
Eso se remonta a los años veinte.

Rendirse **a** alguien:
Me rendí a los encantos de esa mujer.

Renegar **de**:
No deberías renegar de tus ancestros.

Renunciar **a**:
Renuncio a este puesto de director.

Reparar **en**:
No hemos reparado en gastos.

Representar **a**:
Represento a veinte familias de ese condado.

Resentirse **con/contra** alguien **de/por** algo:
Estoy muy resentido con ellos por lo que le hicieron a mi madre.

Resguardarse **de** algo:
Allí podremos resguardarnos de la lluvia.

Resignarse **a** + infinitivo:
Tienes que resignarte a vivir sin ella.

Retar **a** alguien **a**:
He retado a tu hermano a que me demuestre eso.

Retractarse **de**:
No pienso retractarme de lo que dije.

Rezar **a** Dios **por** alguien:
Rezo a Dios por el alma de Antonio.

Rogar **por**:
No quiero rogar por ese puesto.

Romper **con** alguien:
He roto con mi novia.

Rozarse **con**:
Al entrar me rocé con Pablo.

S

Saber **a**:
Este café sabe a agua sucia.

Saciar **de**:
Ellos se saciaron de venganza.

Sacrificarse **por**:
Todos tenemos que sacrificarnos por nuestros hijos.

Sacudirse **de**:
Todas las noches me sacudo de los avatares del trabajo.

Salpicar **con/de**:
Alicia me salpicó de vino.

Salvar **a** alguien **de**:
Salvé a esos chicos de una muerte segura.

Sanar **de**:
Sanarás de esta enfermedad muy pronto.

Seguir **con** algo:
Deberías seguir con tu trabajo.

Sembrar algo **con/de**:
Hemos sembrado estos campos con maíz.

Semejarse **a**:
Esto cada vez se semeja más a algo que ya viví.

Servirse **de** alguien:
Te has servido de mí para obtener eso.

Sincerarse **con**:
Necesito sincerarme con mi mujer.

Sobresalir **por** algo:
Carlos sobresale por su inteligencia.

Sobresaltarse **con/por**:
Me sobresalté con el ruido.

Someterse **a**:
No pienso someterme a tus caprichos.

Sonar **a**:
Eso suena a éxito seguro.

Soñar **con**:
Siempre he soñado con un yate.

Sospechar **de**:
Empiezo a sospechar de ti.

Substituir algo **por** algo:
He substituido estos componentes por esos otros.

Substraerse **a**:
No puedes substraerte a tus responsabilidades.

T

Tachar **a** alguien **de** algo:
Ella tachó a Gerardo de estúpido.

Tardar **en** + infinitivo:
No tardaré en terminar esto.

Templarse **en**:
No te preocupes por eso. Te templarás en la batalla.

Tiritar **de**:
Ella estaba tiritando de frío.

Titubear **en**:
Nunca titubeo en mis decisiones.

Topar **con**:
Hemos topado con algunos problemas.

Trabarse **de**:
El abogado se trabó de nerviosismo.

Traducir **a/en**:
Esta novela ha sido traducida a veinte idiomas.

Traficar **con/en**:
Le han arrestado por traficar con drogas.

Transfigurarse **en**:
Aquella horrible figura se transfiguró en algo siniestro.

Transformarse **en**:
La rana se transformó en príncipe.

Transitar **por**:
No se debe transitar por esa calle a ciertas horas.

Tropezar **con/contra/en**:
Tropecé con Elisa en el supermercado.

Turbar **en**:
El juez me turbó en mi discurso.

U

Ufanarse **con/de**:
Yo me ufano de mi sentido común.

Ungir **con**:
En ese ritual ungen al rey con aceite.

Unir algo/**a** alguien **a/con** algo/alguien:
Dios ha unido a Pablo con María. Que no les separe nadie.

Unirse **a/con**:
Nos vamos a unir a esa empresa para tener mejor acceso al mercado.

Untar **con/de**:
Úntalo de mantequilla por los dos lados.

Usar **de**:
Ellos me usan de criado.

V

Vagar **por**:
Ahora se dedica a vagar por las calles.

Valerse **de**:
Sólo puedes valerte de tus propios medios.

Vanagloriarse **de**:
Felipe se vanagloria de ser el más fuerte de su clase.

Velar **por**:
Mis abogados velan por mis intereses.

Vengarse **de**:
Me vengaré de esa afrenta apenas pueda.

Vindicar **de**:
Algún día me vindicaré de tus ofensas.

Virar **a/hacia**:
El barco viró hacia el norte.

Votar **a/por**:
Yo siempre voto a los liberales.

Z

Zafarse **de**:
Me zafé de mi agresor con un golpe certero.

Zambullirse **en**:
Me gustaría zambullirme en una piscina en este momento.

Answer Key

Chapter 1

Exercise 1
1. están
2. es
3. estoy, soy
4. está/es
5. están
6. es
7. está
8. Es
9. Están
10. Estás

Exercise 2
1. es/está, es/está
2. son
3. están
4. es
5. es
6. estoy, es
7. estamos
8. es/está
9. es
10. es

Exercise 3

1. ¿Cómo están tus padres? ¿Están bien?
2. Correct
3. Correct
4. Está nublado, pero no está lloviendo.
5. no es comprensible
6. yo estoy libre
7. Correct
8. está de pie
9. estás tumbado?
10. Correct

Chapter 2

Exercise 1

1. pasear
2. dejar
3. Entrando/Al entrar
4. terminar
5. terminando, hacer
6. hablar, ser
7. Pintando, conseguir, acabar
8. tener
9. Saliendo/Al salir
10. Al salir/Saliendo

Exercise 2

1. Salir
2. discutir
3. ver
4. haciendo
5. ahorrar, trabajando
6. discutir
7. discutiendo
8. hablar

9. jugar
10. Ser, ser

Exercise 3
1. decirnos
2. diciendo
3. Haciendo
4. dejar, ver
5. seguir, trabajando
6. empujar
7. hablar

Exercise 4
1. cansado
2. hablar
3. invirtiendo
4. encendida
5. hacer
6. rompiendo
7. comprar
8. capacitado
9. poder
10. Tocar

Chapter 3

Exercise 1
1. tengo
2. llega
3. Está estudiando
4. no ceno
5. están saliendo
6. Pasan/Están pasando
7. vas
8. tiene que

Exercise 2
1. Correct
2. Correct
3. Tengo que hacer
4. Creo
5. Vamos a comprar
6. Correct
7. hablas

Exercise 3
1. echo
2. voy
3. estás discutiendo
4. vienes
5. necesito
6. pesa
7. va, tengo
8. Estoy pasando

Exercise 4
1. trabajo, cierra
2. gana
3. habla, está hablando/habla
4. va/está yendo
5. huele, comemos
6. alquilamos
7. tengo/estoy teniendo

Exercise 5
1. cogemos
2. debo
3. desemboca
4. almuerzo
5. Correct
6. Correct
7. están arreglando
8. Correct

Chapter 4

Exercise 1
1. ¿Qué hay?
2. ¿Qué país va a visitar Sara este año?
3. ¿Qué estudian los hermanos de Antonio?
4. ¿Cómo es Elena?
5. ¿Cómo suele ir ella al colegio?
6. ¿Quién vive en esa casa?
7. ¿Cuánto cuesta esta lámpara?
8. ¿A quién vas a invitar?
9. ¿A qué hora tienes que empezar mañana?
10. ¿Quieres comer algo?

Exercise 2
1. ¿no?/¿verdad?
2. ¿quieres?/¿vale?/¿no?
3. ¿quieres?/¿vale?/¿no?
4. ¿vale?/¿de acuerdo?
5. ¿verdad?/¿no?

Chapter 5

Exercise 1
1. recoger
2. hacer
3. lleva
4. apagar
5. dar
6. llevar
7. coger/pillar
8. enseñar
9. llevar
10. recoges

Exercise 2

1. Tienes que
2. va a
3. tiene que
4. Tengo que
5. van a
6. vamos a
7. tienes que

Exercise 3

1. no tenemos que
2. no tenemos que/no tenemos por qué
3. No tengo por qué
4. No tienes por qué
5. No tienes que
6. no tengo por qué
7. no tienes por qué

Chapter 6

Exercise 1

1. se marchan
2. sentarme
3. quedarnos
4. acuestas, me ducho
5. se siente
6. montarse
7. montar
8. le encanta

Exercise 2

1. niega
2. se niega
3. Correct
4. Correct
5. se le puede torcer

6. se dicen
7. Correct
8. no le importa

Exercise 3

1. Se te está arrugando la camisa.
2. A Pedro se le está cayendo el pelo./Se le está cayendo el pelo a Pedro.
3. A Luisa se le están poniendo muy difíciles las cosas./A Luisa se le están poniendo las cosas muy difíciles.
4. A ti no se te puede olvidar mi cumpleaños.
5. Se te está poniendo la cara roja./La cara se te está poniendo roja.

Chapter 7

Exercise 1

1. preparar
2. para
3. dejar
4. pasa/te pasa, lloras/estás llorando
5. prepararte
6. ponerte
7. te pasas
8. abandonar/dejar
9. pasa/está pasando
10. marcharnos

Exercise 2

1. se pone
2. dejar
3. Correct
4. ponerte de pie
5. Correct

Chapter 8

Exercise 1
1. tiene
2. es
3. tiene
4. dando
5. está
6. tomar
7. tener
8. peso

Exercise 2
1. coger(me)/tomar(me)
2. a dar un paseo
3. Correct
4. tomar postre
5. tiene una estatura
6. Correct
7. no voy a tomar nada
8. Correct

Chapter 9

Exercise 1
1. tuve
2. sabía, tenía, decidió
3. preparaba, bañaba/bañó
4. contó, quería, tenía
5. iban
6. terminó, cogió, marchó
7. tropecé, dijeron, esperaban
8. dejó, pasaba
9. bebían, entró, preguntó, había, eran
10. explicó, conducía

Exercise 2

venía, paró, bajó, acercó, estaba/estuvo, pregunté, pasaba/estaba pasando, respondió, llevaba, puse, llevaba, hice, debía, miró, empezó, era, llegué, trataba, bajé, intenté, hacía/estaba haciendo, aparecieron, cogieron, pusieron, era, hacía/estaba haciendo

Chapter 10

Exercise 1

1. discutimos
2. aterran
3. enseñaron
4. preguntó
5. pedí
6. negarte
7. conocemos
8. sabe
9. arriesgarse
10. negaron

Exercise 2

1. Correct
2. podía montar, mi tobillo no estaba
3. preguntó por
4. Correct
5. Correct
6. Correct
7. Niego estar (*not* Me niego a)
8. Correct
9. Correct
10. caminando

Chapter 11

Exercise 1
1. Trabaja allí desde 1990.
2. Correct
3. Estaba hablando
4. no ganamos nada
5. Correct
6. Correct
7. Juan nos conoce
8. Correct

Exercise 2
1. ¿Cuánto tiempo hace que nos esperas/estás esperando?
2. compré
3. estuve estudiando/estudié
4. Ha habido
5. tuvo/tiene/va a tener, mandaste
6. levanté, había, había revuelto/había estado revolviendo
7. llevabas, dejó

Exercise 3
1. he comido/comí
2. tuve
3. He visitado/Visité
4. Tengo
5. sales
6. había terminado
7. había empezado
8. Has estado/Estuviste
9. has obtenido/obtuviste
10. Hubo

Exercise 4
1. No hablo con ella desde hace dos días.
2. Hace un año que no monto en moto.
3. Llevo un año sin beber alcohol.

4. Llevo varios meses sin venir al pueblo.
5. No sé nada de él desde hace más de un mes.

Chapter 12

Exercise 1

1. ganará/va a ganar
2. cenamos/vamos a cenar
3. sale
4. Tengo
5. estaremos
6. habrán terminado
7. Será, suele
8. Quiero/Querría

Exercise 2

1. vas a arrepentir
2. llueve/va a llover
3. habrá/hay, vas/vas a ir
4. empezaremos
5. ha habido
6. puedo/podré, comienza
7. apruebas, compraré
8. tienes

Exercise 3

1. podrías haber echado
2. tendrías que empezar
3. deberías haber puesto
4. podrías haber empezado
5. Tendría que haber tomado
6. deberías estar
7. No deberías hacer
8. podrías haber roto
9. deberías haber dicho
10. podrías haber recogido

Chapter 13

Exercise 1
1. toques
2. dijo
3. termine
4. tiene
5. va
6. vinieras
7. comprobase
8. alquilemos
9. has
10. tengo

Exercise 2
1. acercaran
2. vienen
3. Correct
4. hubiera sabido
5. Correct
6. es culpable
7. Correct
8. Correct
9. estés
10. Correct

Exercise 3
llamó, Quería, hablara, preguntara, gustaba, pareció/parecía, consiguió, colgar/haber colgado, marqué, cogió/cogía, Pensé, había ido/habría ido, entrenaba/estaba entrenando, Decidí, llegué, había marchado, buscara, estuviera, llegar, hacían/estaban haciendo, sentados, Comprendí, tenía, molestara, aprovechando, había visto, fui

Chapter 14

Exercise 1

1. Que la pequeña no vea esa película.
2. No se lo envíes.
3. Que Marco lave los platos esta vez.
4. No nos pagues nada.
5. Préstame el coche esta noche.
6. No se lo traigas mañana.
7. Tráeselo esta noche.
8. No entre sin mi permiso.
9. Estudia para aprobar ese examen.
10. Vámonos ya.

Exercise 2

1. Que no te vayas todavía.
2. Dáselo/Dásela a Elena esta tarde.
3. Correct
4. Pongámonos
5. Que se tumbe la niña en el sofá.
6. Ayúdeme usted, por favor.
7. Correct

Chapter 15

Exercise 1

1. ¿Quieres callarte?
2. Las tiendas no pueden/no deben de estar abiertas.
3. Luisa no se puede haber casado.
4. Sería mejor que fueras al dentista.
5. Podría ser que vinieran esta noche.
6. No he podido terminar el trabajo.
7. ¿Te hace falta ayuda mañana?
8. No les tenías que haber insultado./No les tuviste que insultar./No les deberías haber insultado./No les debiste insultar.

9. No tenías que haber traído tanta cerveza.
10. En Inglaterra debes/tienes que conducir por la izquierda.

Exercise 2

1. Correct
2. estuviera
3. ¿Te echo una mano?
4. Correct
5. Correct
6. No deberías haber hecho eso.
7. cenen
8. fueras
9. Correct
10. Correct

Exercise 3

1. deberías haber comido/debiste comer
2. Podría ser
3. debe de haber llegado
4. deberíamos haber salido/debimos salir
5. funcione
6. tenía que trabajar
7. hizo falta
8. deberías haber estado/debiste estar, Podría haber sido/Pudo ser
9. debíamos de tener
10. podrías haber estudiado/pudiste estudiar

Chapter 16

Exercise 1

1. Correct
2. no te prestará/no te va a prestar
3. necesites
4. fuera más alto
5. viene
6. habría llevado

7. Correct
8. adelgazarías
9. hagas
10. Correct

Exercise 2

1. hubieras desayunado, tendrías
2. llegue, perderemos (type 2 is equally acceptable)
3. pasa/pasaría, perdemos/perdiéramos
4. hubieras hecho, no habrías tenido/no tendrías
5. habría conocido, hubiera ido
6. hace/hiciera, nos quedaremos/quedamos/quedaríamos
7. fuera, mentiría
8. vas, viene
9. vender, esperar
10. hubieras estado

Exercise 3

1. Si Enrique trae el auto, podremos/podemos ir todos juntos./Si Enrique trajera el auto, podríamos ir todos juntos.
2. Si Federico hubiera estado en Londres ese año, habría conocido a Marta.
3. Si Antonio hubiera tenido los utensilios adecuados, habría podido reparar la tubería.
4. Si mis padres no hubieran sabido que iba a haber alcohol en la fiesta, me habrían dado permiso para ir.
5. Si la película no hubiera estado en versión original, lo habría comprendido todo.
6. Si Tomás acepta ese empleo, se mudará a Los Ángeles.
7. Si Javier hubiera tenido un plano, habría podido encontrar la dirección.
8. Si hubiera quedado/hubiera habido cerveza, los clientes no se habrían marchado.
9. Si hubiera estado en Inglaterra, habría aprendido inglés.
10. Si los diques no se hubieran roto, esos pueblos no se habrían inundado.